The Four-Blocks®
Literacy Model

Writing Mini-Lessons for Third Grade:
The Four-Blocks® Model
by
Cheryl M. Sigmon
and
Sylvia M. Ford

Carson-Dellosa Publishing Company, Inc.
Greensboro, North Carolina

Credits

Editors:
Joey Bland
Tracy Soles

Cover Design:
Dez Perrotti

Artist:
Julie Kinlaw

Layout Design:
Joey Bland

ISBN 0-88724-815-2

Acknowledgments

The following teachers, for sharing their ideas and writing samples:

- **Shirley Sexton**, Oasis Academy, BC Grammar #1, Lexington School District Two, West Columbia, South Carolina
- **Tammy Browder**, BC Grammar #1, Lexington School District Two, West Columbia, South Carolina
- **Dianne Fraylick**, Pineview Elementary School, Lexington School District Two, West Columbia, South Carolina
- **Deb Martin**, Southeast Elementary School, North Adams Community Schools, Decatur, Indiana
- **Cindy Wood**, teacher specialist and ERG consultant, Florence, South Carolina
- **Tim Verbootem**, teacher, Department of Defense Schools, Kaiserslautern, Germany

The following school districts, for allowing us to try these lessons in third grade classrooms:

- Hendersonville, NC
- Kokomo, IN
- Decatur, IN
- Lexington, NE
- Danville, VA

And so many other third-grade teachers around the country who have shared with us.

Dedications

To my husband, **Don**, who gives me constant support, and to my daughters, **Melissa** and **Susan**, for providing me with wonderful experiences to write about.

SMF

As always, to my family for their support, inspiration, and love . . .

To my girls: **Ashley**, **Beth**, **Caroline**, and granddaughter, **Meg**

To my guys: **Chuck**, and new grandbaby, **Charles**

To my mom, **Wakefield**, and my sister, **Betty Lou**

To my wonderful in-laws: "**Sig**," **Mona**, and **Marian** (more teachers in the family!)

To those who have gone before: **my dad** and **Freida**, and

To my husband, **Ray**, always beside me.

CMS

Table of Contents

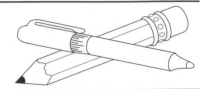

Table of Contents

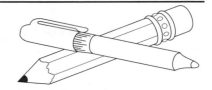

Introduction

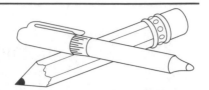

What Is the Writing Block All About?

Welcome to the Writing Block! This is the time of the day in third grade when we all write. We're learning to "talk on paper"—telling about our ideas, our dreams, our fears, and some secrets. We use our imaginations to go anywhere and do anything we want. We write letters and poems, riddles and articles, recipes and stories. We clarify, describe, explain, and invent. We write and then write some more. At some point, we know when to polish. We strike, rewrite, revise, and edit. And, after much effort, we find that we are authors! We pause to celebrate, and then, once again, we begin to write.

In a nutshell, that's what Writers' Workshop is all about! For many of us "baby boomers" who grew up in the Dick–Jane–Sally classrooms, this is quite a different scenario from how we learned about writing. Many of our recollections are more vivid about learning the conventions and correctness of writing than ever actually getting to write. Much time was spent on underlining subjects and verbs, practicing exercise after exercise of where commas should be placed, and diagramming sentences to understand how they should be structured. We had a time of day called **language arts** in which grammar books were the mainstay, a time often completely isolated from other content and certainly not integrated with the other language arts areas of reading, writing, speaking, and listening.

Writing to many of us was something that for many years we didn't feel we were ready to do. We didn't know enough about the mechanics and technicalities to be able to write. We were always preparing for the day we might be ready.

My, how times have changed! Kindergartners now feel confident as writers! They use their wonderful invented spelling to say whatever they wish to say. They write in journals, design stationery to write letters, and even explore informational writing. Being allowed first to become fluent writers, they gradually begin to learn about the conventions that will make their writing clearer and better. Now, by third grade, students are creating truly masterful writings of various genres and are able to talk about their creations as writers should. How envious many of us are of the opportunities in today's classrooms that afford students to develop as writers!

The discovery that grammar, mechanics, usage, genres, organization, voice, etc., can so effectively be taught in the **context of real writing** has breathed life into our classrooms. Students are excited about writing and actually appreciate knowing the mechanics and techniques that will help them to become better writers. Teachers' jobs are so much easier as a result!

Now, let's listen in on a typical Writing Block in one third-grade classroom to see exactly how the Writing Block gets started each day and how teachers teach in a way that models for students what will help them to grow as writers.

It's 9:55 A.M. and the students put away their math books and papers after exploring math problems. The teacher pulls her stool over to the overhead projector and gets her materials ready while the students come to sit on the carpeted area around the projector.

As she does each day, the teacher faces the students as she sits down to begin her mini-lesson. The students know that this is the time when the teacher gets to write, and that if they sit quietly and listen, they'll learn something new that they can use in their own writing. On most days, the teacher talks aloud as she thinks during this writing time. She has explained to the students that she wants them to know how she thinks as she writes, and that is why she shares her thinking out loud with them.

"I'm still thinking about the math that we just finished and some of the things we learned today. A lot of things that we do every day, like math problems, have certain directions or steps that we must follow. I thought today I might try writing some directions. When someone gives me directions, there are two things I really appreciate. The first one is that I think directions are better if they're short and to the point—the fewest words someone can use. Next, I like directions that are clear. They use few words, but they're the best words that could be chosen."

"I think that since we're heading to the cafeteria in just a little while, I'll write directions to get us there. That way you can test my skills at writing directions to see if we end up following them to the cafeteria without a problem!"

The students laugh as Ted remarks, "If you don't write good directions, we might not eat at all today! I'm not sure this is good!" The teacher reassures them that they'll all get to eat even if she fails at writing good directions, and then she begins:

"I'm going to write these directions using numbers to tell the order we'll need to follow. Sometimes we use words like first, second, next, and last, but sometimes we use numbers when there are many different steps." Slowly, as she talks aloud, she writes the following directions:

1. Turn to your left in the hall as you leave the classroom.

2. Walk to the end of the hall and turn right. This is the hall where we go to art.

3. Walk all the way to the main office and turn right again.

4. The third door on the left is the entrance to the cafeteria.

"What do you think? If you had never gone to the cafeteria in our school, do you think these would be good directions? Or, do you think it would help to give you some of what we call 'landmarks' along the way so that you would know you're on the right track to get there?"

Some students reply, "Show us what landmarks are."

"Okay, let me go back and see where landmarks might be helpful. If someone didn't know the main office, they might like knowing that it's the one with the red door and the mailbox beside it." She changes the third sentence to read:

3. Walk all the way to the main office (red door with mailbox outside) and turn right again.

"I think that landmark would be helpful to someone new to our school. Now, let me think if I've been clear and brief in my directions." She reads each sentence again and says, "What about this sentence that says, 'This is the hall where we go to art.' Is it necessary for me to put that in these directions?"

The students respond that they think the directions are clear without that extra sentence, and the teacher agrees. She strikes through the line to omit it.

2. Walk to the end of the hall and turn right. ~~This is the hall where we go to art.~~

Now, they are all satisfied with the way the teacher has written the directions.

"The true test, though, will be whether we all get to the cafeteria today! Jerri, would you be in charge of reading the directions and leading us to the cafeteria later? I'll copy down the directions on a sheet of paper and give them to you."

"Now, it's time for you all to write. You may write about anything you'd like to today, even writing directions if you'd like to try that. Let's hear some of the ideas you've been working on. Any volunteers to share your topics before we get started?"

That's how Writers' Workshop gets started each day during the time that we call the Writing Block. The teacher will model and then each student will have an opportunity to write and to grow in his ability to communicate in written language. On most days, students will write about self-selected topics—whatever they choose to write about. On some days, they'll write a focused piece at the teacher's direction and with the teacher's guidance. Every day, no matter what their topic might be, they will learn, experiment, explore, and grow during this time.

Just because students read more does not necessarily mean they'll read better. The same is true of writing—just because students write more doesn't mean they'll become better writers, even though it's sure to help. To become better readers, students need to learn comprehension skills and strategies that they can apply to get better at reading all types of materials. To become better writers, there is much that students need to learn to communicate more effectively and powerfully for different purposes. As with good reading instruction, good writing instruction requires that teachers teach skills and techniques directly and explicitly. The purpose of this book is to demonstrate how teachers can teach students what they need to learn in a way that makes sense to students and in a way that truly nurtures and supports them.

What makes sense to students is **learning in context**, seeing for themselves the **hows** and **whys** of grammar and mechanics and all that they need to know. Why do we need to know what word is a verb or an adjective? Why does it matter if a comma goes here or there? Why do we need to learn the format of a letter? How are directions written, and what is a good format for writing them? Students need to see this firsthand in "real" writing, not in isolated exercises in a grammar book. The lessons in this book will demonstrate how teaching can be brief and to the point, but still serve as an illustration of how and why a skill is useful in writing.

Writing is a critical component of any balanced language arts program, whether or not Four Blocks is the specific design of that program. Writing is how students figure out what reading is all about and how they learn about one of literacy's most valuable tools—the power of the written word.

What Is a Mini-Lesson?

The term "mini" means **brief**, always within the attention span of third-graders. The lessons in this book are designed to last approximately 10 minutes daily. Some of the lessons are a series of multiple-day lessons, which are necessary to model for students since they also will continue their writing over multiple days. The Writing Block should always allow more time for students to write than the time allowed for the teacher's modeling and for the sharing that may occur at the conclusion.

The mini-lesson should be direct and explicit, with the teacher focusing on one particular aspect of writing. The lesson allows the teacher the opportunity to **show** the students how and why a skill or technique is used in the context of writing. Once students see how a skill or technique is used and why they might use it, they translate this into their own writing when needed. The focus of the lesson will be some curriculum item that is important for third-graders to be aware of in their writing: composing notes and letters; using commas; combining short, choppy sentences; using the descriptive mode of writing; or a number of other lessons that will help students grow as writers.

The mini-lesson is not necessarily interactive. Sometimes the students only listen quietly to the teacher talking aloud. Occasionally, the teacher will ask questions of the students or elicit responses of different sorts to help the students process what's being taught. However, this is the **time for the teacher to do the teaching**. The students will have their chance to write and make decisions **after** the mini-lesson.

How Many Mini-Lessons?

There will be one central focus for the mini-lesson each day during the Writing Block. Other elements of writing are taught peripherally or incidentally, not stressed as the main lesson is. For example, a teacher may be teaching a mini-lesson on writing letters. As a part of the modeling, the teacher might include in the think-aloud such things as: indenting to start the letter, how to abbreviate the name of the state, capital letters at the beginnings of sentences, and margins. The repetition of basic elements will serve as a constant reminder to students that they should do this in their writing.

In this book, there are a variety of mini-lesson topics, as well as suggestions for follow-up lessons. Rarely would you want to teach something and not reinforce it with additional lessons. So, in all, you have more mini-lessons than you should need to use throughout the year!

How Are Mini-Lessons Selected?

The mini-lessons in this book are based on frequently-taught curricula for third grade. The lessons are arranged into three general categories, based on the point in the year that may be most appropriate for you to introduce those lessons. The section **Early in Third Grade–Getting Started** offers lessons that will help you to teach and review the basics of grammar, mechanics, the writing process, and routines that students will need to know. Suggestions are made about which of these basics you may wish to include in your Editor's Checklist. After you teach one of these basic lessons and feel that your students can be accountable for this in their own writing, you may wish to add this element to a checklist displayed in your classroom as a resource and reminder for your students. This checklist is not the criteria to which students will be accountable for their final published pieces. This checklist is only a list of basics that will make the students' writing easier for them to read back or easier for you or peers to read if it's shared. Keeping the checklist short will help students remember it easily and apply these basics to all of their rough-draft writing.

The **Getting Started** lessons in the beginning of the year will also allow time for students to develop fluency in their writing before they attempt to incorporate new and different ideas.

The next section, **Most of Third Grade–Continuing to Write**, provides lessons to use after students have learned the basics. These lessons will help students grow in their abilities to communicate in writing. They'll explore writing for various purposes, for different audiences, and with greater clarity. With these lessons, students will understand that writing is more than editing or correctness. They'll come to understand that "clean" writing isn't even necessarily good writing.

Finally, there are lessons in the section, **Later in Third Grade–Getting Better!**, for classrooms that are ready to advance to more complex lessons. These are lessons that polish writing and move into craft, style, and complexity. Not all third-grade classrooms will be ready for these lessons. Whether or not these particular selections should be used is left to the discretion of the teacher with consideration of the maturity of the students and the readiness for more sophistication in their writing.

You probably have a curriculum that guides you in knowing what is necessary for third-graders to know about writing. If you're a teacher using this book for your lessons, you'll want to be sure to check the suggested lessons with whatever local or state curriculum you have to be sure all of your items are covered. You'll need to add the items not included that will offer perfect alignment with what your students need to know this year.

In addition to consulting your curriculum guide in concert with this book, you'll want to be guided by your students' needs as determined by their writing. As you read what they've written, make notes of what would add to their knowledge of writing so that you can make that a part of your mini-lessons, too. This book should make it easy for you to plug your own curriculum into model lessons.

How Do You Get Started?

Getting started with your lessons takes a minimum of planning, especially with this book as your guide for the mini-lesson portion. You'll want to **find a comfortable place** to write every day. It will need to be a place where your writing will be in clear view of all of your students. Using an overhead projector and screen would be ideal so that everyone can see clearly. The other major advantage to using an overhead projector is that you can model everything you want students to know about writing—even the posture of a writer (if you're able to pull up a chair beside the projector). This also allows you to face the students as you make decisions and think aloud.

Gather a variety of writing materials for your use: transparencies or paper, dark markers that will make your pieces visible for your students, and colored markers to highlight what you're focusing on. You'll want to save many of the pieces you write, so prepare a folder in which you can keep your work. Returning to an earlier piece to revise or edit is valuable to teach your students.

Next, plan what you'll write about daily and what your mini-lesson will be. This book will help you with that. Most of the lessons in this book have sample lessons written. If you wish to use them, you can easily change names and places to personalize them for your own. Know where you're heading each day when you write. Have a specific purpose for your writing model.

Be brave! If you currently lack confidence in yourself as a writer (as many teachers admit!), just take a deep breath and try it. Modeling in front of students may be difficult in the beginning, but it will get easier. Soon you'll think nothing of it! In fact, keep in mind that you really should keep your writing as simple as possible, especially in the beginning. If your writing is too grand or exemplary, you may actually "turn off" your students. Write about your family members, your childhood, ordinary, every-day kinds of things, and then your students will know that they have things to write about, too! Take advantage of sharing something about yourself during this time.

What Will Students Write About?

It's important for you to realize that students don't have to write about what you've written about each day. Nor do they **always** have to apply whatever they've just been taught. If you've taught your students how to use commas in a series of words, it's not necessary to have them write something right away that requires them to use ten commas. If you do that, you usually won't get quality writing from your students. They'll only be writing towards that objective and not writing with creativity and imagination. Trust that when you model, they'll absorb.

Occasionally, you may wish to ask that students practice something you've taught. You'll want to do that sparingly and in the context of real writing. This focused or guided writing will occur more often as students move into upper grades.

In the Writing Block, you'll reinforce what you've taught by reteaching it, maybe several times, gauging how often by what you see in your students' writing. The extension lessons in this book will help you to plan these follow-up lessons. You can also take advantage of formal and informal conference time, which will allow you the opportunity to encourage the use of the skills and techniques you've been teaching.

So, on most days, your students will write about whatever they want to write about. On some days, though, you'll say to them, "Today and tomorrow, we're going to work together on writing letters, and then on Thursday you can get back to whatever you've been working on." That'll be the time that you spend guiding them through a lesson that must be taught and practiced immediately. Your students will understand this, but they'll appreciate the time to get back to their own writing as well.

What Is the Four-Blocks® Literacy Model?

These mini-lessons are designed to fit perfectly into the Writing Block of the Four-Blocks® Literacy Model. The lessons, however, are certainly not exclusive to Four-Blocks classrooms and can be used with any classroom using a Writers' Workshop approach. The Writing Block is just one of the Four Blocks which comprise the Four-Blocks framework. Four Blocks is an approach used to teach students how to read and grow in their knowledge of literacy and language.

Four Blocks is a comprehensive language arts program based on the work of its creators, Drs. Patricia Cunningham and Dorothy Hall. The foundation of Four Blocks is that reading can be taught without labeling and dividing children homogeneously. Experts agree that there are four major approaches that can be used to teach children how to read. Instead of picking and choosing one of the approaches as "the" way to teach children to read, Four-Blocks teachers present a balanced method, taking all four of the major approaches and exposing all children in heterogeneous settings to all four approaches each day at the primary grades. Because students all have different learning styles, personalities, and bring different experiences to the classroom, there must be a variety of ways in which they will learn best to read. So, to address this diversity, Four Blocks is multilevel, meeting the needs of high-, average-, and low-achieving students in the same setting.

One of the Four Blocks is the **Self-Selected Reading** Block. Based on the research that says children who read the most are the children who read the best, a minimum of 30 minutes a day is devoted to Self-Selected Reading (Cunningham, Hall, and Gambrell, 2002). The teacher starts this block by reading aloud to the students to motivate them and to introduce them to a variety of literature. Then, students read while the teacher conferences with some students, engaging them in a book chat to further motivate them and to encourage them to read. Sharing time may be available at the conclusion of this block that allows students some brief time to share what they've been reading. For more information on Self-Selected Reading, see *Self-Selected Reading the Four-Blocks® Way* by Patricia M. Cunningham, Dorothy P. Hall, and Linda B. Gambrell (Carson-Dellosa, 2002).

Another of the blocks is the **Guided Reading** Block, 30–40 minutes devoted to teaching comprehension skills and strategies and allowing students to practice and apply them. This block usually begins with the teacher instructing the whole group, connecting them to the text they'll read—building vocabulary and background knowledge, making predictions, and setting a purpose for reading. Then, the teacher decides on the best way to support all readers in the class through various formats—partner reading, ERT, book club groups, Three-Ring Circus, choral reading, independent reading, etc. Closure allows the students to come back together to check their successes with the skills they were working with that day. For more information on Guided Reading see *Guided Reading the Four-Blocks® Way* by Patricia M. Cunningham, Dorothy P. Hall, and James W. Cunningham (Carson-Dellosa, 2000).

A third block is the **Working with Words** Block, giving students time to explore spelling and decoding. During this time, students spend approximately 10 minutes working with high-frequency words—those words that students encounter often in their reading and need to use in their writing. An additional 15–20 minutes is spent on another activity to teach more about spelling and decoding, usually concentrating on patterns of words and language. This time might include well-known activities like Making Words, Sorts and Hunts, What Looks Right, Guess the Covered Word, and Reading and Writing Rhymes. For more information on Working with Words, see *Month-by-Month Phonics for Third Grade* by Patricia M. Cunningham and Dorothy P. Hall (Carson-Dellosa, 1998).

The fourth block is the one partially addressed in this book, the **Writing** Block. This 30–40 minutes begins with the teacher modeling writing for approximately 10 minutes, during which a mini-lesson is taught. Then, students have an opportunity to write, mostly on self-selected topics and sometimes on assigned or focused writing. Teachers find time to have individual conferences with students while all students are writing. The teacher usually targets the whole class during the mini-lesson, but the conference is the time that the teacher can grow students individually from wherever they are in their writing development. Some sharing time is included in the closure of this block to allow students to talk with their peers about what they've written.

Together, these are the Four Blocks. They offer a balanced literacy program to students and a wonderful management system for teachers planning their instruction and their time. Besides being a great organizational method, this is a framework that truly embraces all children regardless of their reading ability level. Students learn to nurture and support each other—truly a community of learners! They learn not simply to tolerate their differences, but truly to appreciate those differences that they share.

For more information on the Four-Blocks® Literacy Model, see *The Teacher's Guide to the Four-Blocks®* by Patricia M. Cunningham, Dorothy P. Hall, and Cheryl M. Sigmon (Carson-Dellosa, 1999).

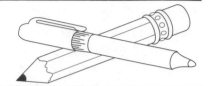

Early in Third Grade–Getting Started

Mini-Lesson Focus: Beginning to Write

In the beginning of the year, the first goal you'll tackle in the Writing Block is to get students to write. This sounds so simple, and yet, it's much easier said than done! This is the time during which students may hesitate to write immediately, may lack confidence that they have ideas worthy of writing about, and definitely suffer complete writer's block on many days. We must get them started writing, though, and so we encourage them daily. At this point, we keep the writing process and our explanation of it **simple**.

Model a short piece of writing. Start by talking aloud about the topic choices you might make, "What do I want to write about today? I could write about something I did with my family this summer that was fun. I might write about a movie I saw last weekend. Or, since it's early in the school year, I've been thinking about how much I enjoy getting a new year started. That's what I want to write about today!"

Beginning a School Year

I really get excited about starting a new school year every August. Why is it so exciting for me. There are a number of reasons I love it so much. For me, it's a chance to try new things that I've been thinking about during the summer. I usualy read lots of professional books during my vacation time to get new ideas for my classroom. Sometimes I attend a seminar or two to learn new things. I take the best of the ideas that I've learned to try on my 25 new guiny pigs—my students!

After you've written, explain to students, "This is what you'll be doing each day—writing." Then, explain the following short process to them.

You might add, "Each day during the Writing Block, you're expected to write. On most days you'll write on self-selected topics—anything you want to write about! Also, on most days, you are *not* required to finish a piece within the 15–20 minutes you'll have to write, and you can write on a piece for as many days as you need to. For the piece I've started today, I'll probably choose to write a little more to tell you other reasons that I love to get each new school year started."

Other Ideas for Beginning to Write

- Even before introducing the Editor's Checklist, you'll want to encourage students to read over what they've written to be sure it makes sense. Using the previous model lesson, the teacher might say, "Boys and girls, I want to be sure to read over what I've written. I want to make sure it makes sense. As the teacher reads, she finds a question mark should be used instead of a period at the end of the second sentence. She changes it. She looks at **usualy** and says, "Oops! I think 'usually' should have been spelled with two l's. Let me change that. I think I've misspelled 'guinea' (**guiny**), so let me circle that word and check it later. Now, it is clean and easy to read back!"

- Also explain to students that, "Any day during the Writing Block, when you finish a piece and read back over it, you can choose between a couple of options. First, you can continue to work on that piece, reading back over it and deciding if it's the best it can be. If it's not, some changes can be made before moving on to a new piece. Second, you can choose to move from one piece to another after the quick-edit is complete."

This is the short writing process for early in the year:

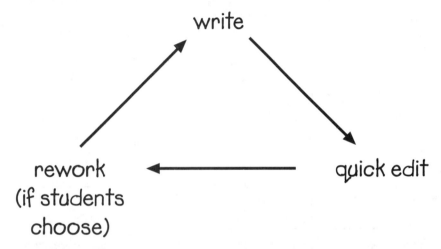

- You might try setting a timer to go off before the last five minutes of the writing time. Announce that all students may want to skim over whatever they've written. This will prepare students for the advent of the formal Editor's Checklist which is introduced early in the year.

Mini-Lesson Focus: Coming up with Ideas (Using a Jot List)

Children need many ideas to draw from when choosing a topic. Preparing a jot list of topics early in the year will allow for a more efficient Writing Block. If children talk about and share their ideas, then the writing is easier.

Tell students, "When I try to think of something to write about, I might play around with ideas in my head. If I do that, then I have to do the same thing every time I try to think of a topic for my writing. I think it would be better to jot down these ideas as I think of them. I could really be organized if the topics were written on a form. Why don't we work on this in our lesson for today?"

Using the overhead projector, share a transparency with nine boxes of categories for writing. Model how to jot down ideas in each box. Talk about ideas in each category that you plan to write about this year.

Ideas for Writing

Pets	Family	Friends
Shama	Don	Ray
Prissy	Melissa	Cheryl
Brandy	Susan	Docia
	Granny	Joe
	Sonny	Linda
Foods	**Sports**	**Games**
pizza	football	board games
steak	basketball	video games
chicken	soccer	card games
holiday meals	baseball	dominoes
foods at the fair	tennis	kickball
desserts	hockey	jump rope
Holidays	**Favorite Places**	**Vacations**
Valentine's Day	seashore	Charleston, SC
Thanksgiving	mountains	New York City
Christmas	restaurants	Disney World
Hanukkah	my house	New Orleans, LA
Easter		my aunt's house

Give each child a blank copy of the **Ideas for Writing** form. Set a timer for 10 minutes. "Talk about each of these categories with a partner. Then, I will reset the timer for 10 more minutes. As you talk, jot down topic ideas in each block."

Allow the children to share their ideas. Encourage each child to add to his list when he hears a topic shared about something he knows. Provide a space in a writing folder or notebook for this idea jot list.

Other Ideas for Coming up with Ideas

- Provide a mini-lesson on using childhood and family memories for writing topics. You can also get the family involved with writing to stimulate topics for the students to write about. Send home a letter asking parents to talk with their child about family memories, events, and traditions. You may want to provide a form which can be used to gather this information. The form can be filed in the student's writing folder as a handy resource for topics. Be sure to provide a mini-lesson showing students how the form can be used to choose topics.

- Another graphic organizer that can be used to list topics is a chart like the one on page 16, using letters of the alphabet. Provide a mini-lesson early in the year where the chart is used to list topics that the teacher might write about. Refer to the chart throughout the year as you add topics and to help select topics.

A aardvarks antennae	B baseball bats	C chameleons cats cars
D dogs dragons	E elephants eagles eggs	F frogs firefighters

- Early in the year, select a small bulletin board or area in the room to serve as a "Graffiti Board" for writing topics. Cover the area with bulletin board paper and write the title, **Topics to Write About**, across the top. Early in the year, write suggestions on the board as you read or discuss something interesting to write about. Invite the students to help throughout the year by adding ideas to the board. Occasionally, choose a topic from the board for your mini-lesson.

Mini-Lesson Focus: Coming up with Ideas (Class Reporter)

Quite often students will find that coming up with an idea for their writing is an excruciating task, made even more difficult when the writing is flowing around them. Peer pressure can definitely add to that dreaded disease—writer's block! Using the class reporter method to connect with a topic can often solve this problem.

"Writer's block is something that every writer suffers with occasionally—even teachers! There will be days when it's really tough to come up with a good idea to write about. Today I'm going to share a technique for handling this problem."

The one you'll model for them today is called the Class Reporter, and you'll model how it works.

"On a day like today, when I have writer's block, I'll get started with my writing by pretending to be a reporter in the classroom, observing what's going on around me. Let me look around and see what others are doing during the Writers' Workshop. It looks like Pat and Jeffrey are publishing books in the publishing center. Let me peek over and see what Rodney, our class's pet gerbil, is doing. He's providing some entertainment running on his wheel. I'll make some notes about what I see and hear during this time."

A rule must be shared with the students as this technique is introduced: **The class reporter cannot "tattle" on others!**

Tell the students: "Each time you record your observations, you'll want to make a connection to an idea for a good piece to write about. You can do this in your head as you go, or you might find it easier to make notes or draw pictures to help you come up with your good idea or what to write about.

"When a personal connection is made, your writing will take a life of its own! It works almost every time! When your 'real' piece starts, you can choose one of these: strike through all the writing that provided the path to your new idea and just keep writing; start your 'real' writing on a clean page of paper; or draw a line after your class reporting and continue with your new piece."

Start by modeling: "Boys and girls, I'm going to pretend that I'm stumped for a writing topic today and that our writing time has begun. I'm going to use the Class Reporter technique for coming up with an idea. I begin to look around the room and write whatever I see…"

> Liz is erasing a section of her writing. Mrs. Reeves, the librarian, just walked by our door. She was pushing a book cart stacked high with books.

Stop and think aloud: "I could write about a book I've just read. I'm not sure I want to do that. Think I'll keep writing for now."

> Joey is reading over his work as he chews on his blue pencil. Yolanda is working with Pat in the corner. I think they're revising Yolanda's last piece of writing before she has a conference. Yolanda's last story that she shared with the class was a fantasy about living on the moon. We just learned some interesting things about the moon in science.

Think aloud: "Aha! It might be fun to write either about why the moon might be a fun place to live or why it wouldn't be such a good place to live! That's it! I might even use some of the facts we learned in my writing. Now, where's my science book so that I can get started? Let me draw a double line here to show that I'm now ready to write my 'real' piece!"

Other Ideas for Coming up with Ideas

- Some teachers have posters to aid students who are at a loss for ideas to write about. Here are two poster ideas:

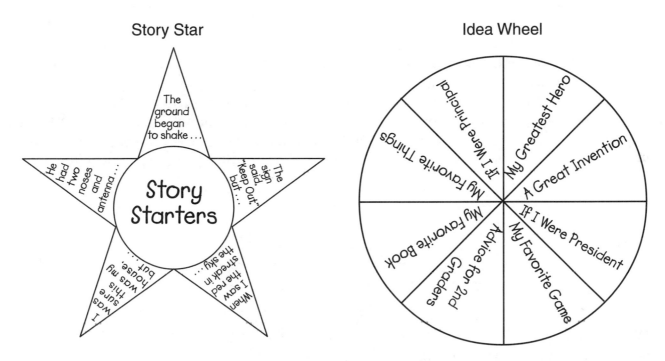

Story Star   Idea Wheel

- You might keep a jar in the room filled with slips of paper on which you've jotted ideas/topics/first lines to get students started with their own writing. You won't want the students to rely too heavily on the jar, but everyone catches writer's block at some time. You might give the students a ticket that they can redeem once a month or once every couple of weeks for a draw from the jar.

- Students may get ideas from a monthly bulletin board that you create. The bulletin board can reflect the season, special events, holidays, or unusual celebrations (National Pizza Day, National Juggling Day, Accordion Awareness Month, etc.). You may want to include a Word Wall that lists words associated with the events highlighted on the bulletin board.

- You might keep a small space reserved for a few unusual objects or pairs of objects that students can use to stimulate their imagination—army boots with a flower stuck inside of one, a baseball cap with a tube of lipstick, a glove with two fingers cut off, a flower pot with a baby rattle, etc. Model how students can look at these objects and make up stories about how they've come to be paired together or what they symbolize.

Mini-Lesson Focus: Extending Writing over Multiple Days

Just as students in third grade have learned to sustain their interest in reading a book over multiple days, now they will become interested in working on the same piece of writing over a number of days. Students at this grade need to realize that quality writing isn't defined by the length of the composition (hence the shouts of "How long does it have to be?"). They need to learn that a composition needs to be as long as it takes to say what needs to be said—no longer, no shorter. Many students who haven't been in Writers' Workshops may be conditioned to write one piece per day on an assigned topic. Just being allowed the freedom to write about what they want to and for as long as they want to, however, doesn't always come naturally to students. As with everything else, teachers must model exactly what they want students to do.

Day One

In your model lesson for the first day, write a composition that you intentionally don't complete. Your composition will extend over a period of two or more days. For example, you might start on Day One by doing some mental planning or by completing a quick graphic organizer to outline what you'll write about. In mental planning, you might say, "Since it's snowing today, I can't help but think about snowy days when I was your age. That's what I think I'll write about today. I'll share with you some of the things that I did when I was nine years old. I'll want to write about the games we played and the things we cooked with snow as our main ingredient! Let me get started!"

Snow Fun

When I was growing up, I lived in a state where it snowed only once or twice each winter. When it snowed, we always made the best of the little time we would have for what we called "snow fun." All of the kids in our neighborhood had a favorite game and even a special recipe that we looked forward to on those particular days. As soon as the flakes began to fall, we knew to run and meet as early as possible at the big tree at the end of the block.

When you've written for the amount of time you usually write within one day, stop and comment, "I'll need to stop here today. That's all I have time for. I have much more that I want to add to this, but I'll have to continue it tomorrow."

Complete your quick edit. You might also find something to focus on for a mini-lesson beyond the larger purpose of modeling multiple-day writing. In the above sample, this teacher might emphasize the use of introductory clauses, pointing out how much they look like sentences but how they can't stand alone ("When I was growing up,…" "When it snowed,… " "As soon as the flakes began to fall,…"). Another idea for a mini-lesson might be why and how the quotation marks are used for a term like "snow fun."

Day Two

On the second day, you'll need to show students how you reconnect to a piece of writing that has been started. Think out loud as you get started, "I have so much more to tell you about this. I've got to be sure, though, that I've remembered exactly what I was writing yesterday. I need to read it back carefully."

Read the first day's composition aloud, then think aloud about how to continue with your writing. "What do I need to tell about now? I've told you that we loved to play a certain game and cook with the snow, but I've only introduced the idea. I haven't really told you any details yet. Let me start with our favorite games." Then, reconnect to your previous day's thoughts, and continue to write.

A second paragraph might look like…

> The first game was always a fierce fight with the boys against the girls. If enough snow had fallen, we used it to build forts. Sometimes trees became our fortresses. We allowed a certain amount of time to gather snowballs and stockpile them in our areas. Then, when time was called, we began to hurl our weapons at each other. Sometimes we kept score of how many of the enemy we hit. Sometimes we didn't care. We just threw our snowballs, laughing and screaming the whole time!

Day Three

On the next day, return to your composition, reading back over it and reconnecting your thoughts. For this lesson, the teacher might say, "Now, I've written my paragraph about a game we played, but I haven't written yet about the cooking we did. I guess that's what I need to write about today. I'll need to indent since my thoughts in each paragraph support a different idea about 'snow fun.'"

A third paragraph on this day might look like…

> Cooking with the snow was another of our favorite "snow fun" events. Just as the snow began to fall, we placed tin pie pans outside on the picnic table. As they filled with fresh snow, we brought them in to make snow ice cream. Our recipe was simple: a dash of vanilla, a sprinkle of sugar, and a little milk to make it creamy. We stirred it until it turned to slush and then gobbled it up! Yum!

Day Four

The think-aloud continues as in the previous days: "Well, let me look over what I've written to see if I need to add anything else. In the first paragraph I talked briefly about the topic and told that I wanted to write about a favorite snow game and a favorite snow recipe. In the second paragraph, I described the game I liked best. In the third paragraph, I gave the snow ice cream recipe. I think that's about all I wanted to talk about in detail. Now, I think I need to write a closing paragraph so that I'm not ending too abruptly. I suppose I could just tell again that I have very fond memories of these things. Let me get started."

The final paragraph might look like…

> Snow days aren't quite the same any longer for me. Getting hit now with a snowball doesn't sound like so much fun, and pollution has made eating snow ice cream dangerous for us. I will always remember, though, the fun that snow brought to me as a young girl. When I see the snow fall now, there is a warm memory of days gone by, and I feel the urge to grab a pie pan and head outside!

Remind the students that, "The wonderful thing about having a Writers' Workshop is that you can usually write for as many days as you want to on a certain piece. You don't have to rush and finish a piece each day. You can write just like your favorite authors do!"

Mini-Lesson Focus: Formatting

You will surely want to set some basic parameters for your students to use in their daily writing. Whatever your basic standards of formatting are, teach them directly during your mini-lesson time and explain the reason for requiring them.

With whatever you're writing for your mini-lesson, include the basics in your daily think-aloud—what you're including and why you're including it. You will be the one to decide what's most important for your students. Choose any or all from below:

Student's Names

Where?

When modeling, you must put your own name on your drafts to model where students will put theirs. When students use lined paper, saying "in the upper right hand corner" seems to leave a wide range of possibilities that may lack the uniformity you desire. Many teachers tell students to use the top line and to start writing exactly in the middle of the line and not beyond the right margin. "Okay, I'm going to get started by putting my name on my paper. I'll start here on the top line in between the margin lines. My name will fit perfectly from here to the right margin."

Why?

Students always seem to be curious about why you ask them to do certain things, and, as often as we can, we offer this rationale. With names, you'll want students to know that often papers can get mixed up, and you wouldn't want to lose something that they worked so hard on. Remind them that since their names are the first thing to go on the paper, they should write things that they'll take pride in connecting to their names.

Date

Where?

The choice is yours; however, many teachers ask students to write the date (including day, month, and year) just below their names. You may want to ask students to write out the month, abbreviate the month, or to use numerals for the complete date.

Why?

Dates are especially important if samples of writing are collected to show individual progress over time. Both you and the students will want to see early, midyear, and late-year samples, and hopefully, the growth that has taken place. Dates on papers may also be used to determine when students have written an adequate amount to be considered ready to publish. Usually a certain number of pieces are required before publication is considered. Not everything should be published, because students need to learn to distinguish good from mediocre pieces of their own writing.

Margins

Where?

Teach students to observe the left and right margins on their papers when they're using lined notebook paper. Both margin lines, of course, are red vertical lines. The left margin is much easier than the right to see clearly since the right margins are actually printed on the backsides of notebook paper. The margin lines are to be regarded as "fences" within which the words are to stay.

You don't need to be as picky with margins on rough drafts as with final drafts. Decide for yourself how strict you want to set the margin rules for rough draft writing. Many students don't regard any margins. This makes their writing difficult to read and less acceptable as they go up through the grades.

Students are to start words at the left margin and to write until they come to the right margin. At that point, they'll either stop and take the next word down to the following line, or, in final drafts and in formal writing, they'll hyphenate a word that reaches the line but can't be completed. Let students know that they cannot choose where they'd like to hyphenate words. The hyphenations must occur at the syllable divisions. If they're dealing with a short word, they should just carry it to the next line. Long words can be hyphenated. When in doubt, just carry the word down.

Why?
Observing margin lines greatly helps the reader of the composition. Also, if margin lines are observed, then room remains for revisions that may need to occur.

Writing on Every Other Line (optional)

Where?
Many teachers like for students to write only on every other line of their notebook paper.

Why?
Having space between lines of text helps both the writer and the reader. Especially as many students in third grade are practicing their cursive handwriting or refining their fine motor skills, sometimes letters and words tend to run together if written on single lines. Skipping lines in between helps greatly. Also, as students become more and more adept at revisions, they'll have much more room to do their revisions.

Cursive or Manuscript?

This great debate continues! You'll be the one to determine whether students can write using manuscript or whether they must practice cursive during this time. Advice would be to allow manuscript or whatever students are most comfortable using during rough draft writing. The purpose is to get good ideas on paper and not to concentrate on handwriting as much during this time. Final drafts may be another story since they're more formal.

Note: All of these basic formats should be modeled daily as a part of the teacher think-aloud.

Start the Editor's Checklist:

1.   I have included my name and the date.

Mini-Lesson Focus: Using Capital Letters Appropriately

In third grade, students should be held accountable for the correct use of capital letters. By this time, the students have had instruction in using capital letters at the beginnings of sentences, when writing proper nouns (names of specific people, places, and events), and in titles. This mini-lesson will be to add the appropriate use of capital letters to the Editor's Checklist.

Talk about what you will write about: "As I tell you about my plane trip to California, I should be sure to use capital letters where needed. I visited lots of different places while I was there. I need to remember that I always have to capitalize names of places. Names of people and events should also be capitalized. When we add this rule to the Editor's Checklist, it will make it easier for me to remember this rule!" (Intentionally omit capital letters where needed.)

my trip to california

last month I flew to the state of california. It was an exciting trip because I had not been there before. The plane trip lasted four hours so I watched a movie during the flight. After arriving in los angeles, california, I got on a tour bus to santa monica, beverly hills, bel-air, venice beach, and disney land. The tour guide's name was Mr. fisher, and he really knew a lot about the area. He made sure I was present for the holiday at the beach festival. I really enjoyed my trip to california and I look forward to returning in the spring.

Guide the students in editing the modeled passage for correct use of capital letters. Circle the words that should be capitalized.

As the students write, they are responsible for using capitals correctly. After being taught the additional reasons for the use of capital letters, the students will be held accountable for this part of the Editor's Checklist.

Add to the Editor's Checklist:

    2.   I have used capital letters where appropriate.

Other Ideas for Using Capital Letters Appropriately

- Play "Rounding Up the Capitals." Tell the students to use colored pencils to circle all of the capital letters in a piece of their writing. They may then partner with a peer and tell why the capital was used (for example, beginning of a sentence, the pronoun I, proper nouns, titles, etc.).

- Sometimes it is appropriate to make a graphic organizer **after** writing to analyze proper use of conventions. The children can fill in the appropriately capitalized words from their writing in a graphic organizer such as the one below. Tell the children to justify their use of capitals to a partner.

Title	First Word of Each Sentence	Pronoun "I"	Specific People	Specific Places	Specific Events

- Give the children old greeting and holiday cards and colored pencils. Have them circle where capital letters are used correctly with one color and where capital letters are needed with another color. They should then share their findings with a partner.

Mini-Lesson Focus: Using Correct Ending Punctuation

By third grade, student writers should be able to use correct ending punctuation. Using correct ending punctuation is included on most classroom Editor's Checklists.

Talk about the mini-lesson focus: "Let's think back to the lessons we have learned about ending punctuation. Remember that a period is used to end a sentence that makes a statement or gives a command that is not an exclamation. A question mark is used at the end of a direct question, and an exclamation point is used to express strong feelings. We are very good at remembering to add punctuation in our writing. You will see a paragraph that was written by a third-grade student where the ending punctuation has been omitted. We will enjoy solving the mystery by deciding whether a period, question mark, or exclamation point is needed."

Make a transparency of a piece of writing where ending punctuation is missing. Share with the class how important these punctuation marks are. This will be evident as you read through the sentences with no expression. Leaving a space at the end of each complete thought will ensure that the focus of this lesson is on which type of punctuation to use and not on where it should be used. This type of mini-lesson engages each child and makes an impact on the importance of using the correct ending punctuation.

About Fall

I like fall__ I like fall because you can jump in the leaves__ Wow__ It is fun__ Do you like to play in the leaves__ When I go outside I see people raking leaves__ Fall has many changes__ People go to the fair__ There are some festivals__ Fall is the best season of the year__

After reading the piece of writing, involve students in deciding what types of punctuation are needed.

As this skill is added to the Editor's Checklist, tell the children, "Be sure that correct ending punctuation is part of what you check for in your writing."

Add to the Editor's Checklist:

       3.   I have used correct ending punctuation.

Other Ideas for Using Correct Ending Punctuation

- Children enjoy editing when they are allowed to use motivating tools such as colored pencils. They will have great fun going on an "Ending Punctuation Scavenger Hunt!" Using a piece of their writing, have them circle the periods in blue, the question marks in green, and the exclamation points in red. Then, tell them to reread their writing to be sure that they used correct ending punctuation.

- Select a passage from a piece of literature. Make a transparency of the selection and cover the ending punctuation with self-stick notes. Play "Guess the Covered Punctuation." Have students justify their guesses, and then uncover to see if they agreed with the author.

- Allow the children to read their writing into a tape recorder using correct expression. As they listen to the recording, it may be more evident whether the punctuation used is correct or needs to be changed.

Mini-Lesson Focus: Writing Sentences that Express Complete Thoughts

Writing sentences with complete thoughts is an essential skill for successful communication. Growth in this skill requires extensive practice. Sentences must express complete thoughts. The classroom Editor's Checklist may include this skill.

Think aloud: "As I think of sentences to write, I have to make sure that they are complete. My sentences have to answer the questions *who*, *what*, and *what happened*. If only part of the question is answered, then my sentence is not complete."

Model writing sentences that describe what you see when you look outside your classroom window. Include two or three incomplete sentences, such as:

Outside Our Window

When I look out the window of our classroom, I can see many things. The trees. And the birds. The basketball court is full of children playing. Children are. Many cars are parked on the street. There are so many sights outside our window.

Explain that a sentence must express a complete thought. Discuss each sentence in the paragraph. Identify and underline the three incomplete sentences. Talk about the missing action. A person, place, or thing is the subject of the statement or question. To be complete, the sentence must also contain an action or being word.

Ask the students to add words to change the three incomplete sentences into complete ones.

For example:

The trees are blowing in the wind.

The birds are flying in the sky.

Children are running around the track.

Add to the Editor's Checklist:

4.   I have used sentences that express complete thoughts.

Other Ideas for Writing Sentences that Express Complete Thoughts

• Have the students write on any topic of their choice. Allow a few minutes at the conclusion of the writing time to direct students to read each sentence of their stories to see if all of their sentences are complete and make sense.

• Provide a form that can be used to list the person, place, or thing and the action or being word in each sentence. The student can select a previously written piece to analyze.

Person, Place, or Thing	Action or Being Word
1. box	is
2. crayons	are

• You can also model writing a mini-lesson that focuses on the description of an object in the classroom or something that can be seen outside the classroom window. You should include some complete and incomplete sentences. The students should work with you to correct the incomplete sentences so that they express complete thoughts.

Mini-Lesson Focus: Staying Focused

Early in the year, you'll want to concentrate on having students become more fluent in their writing. If they've already participated in a Writing Block or Writers' Workshop for a couple of years, they'll need little, if any, time by third grade to feel confident as writers. Once they become self-assured as writers, then you'll slowly help them to grow in their abilities to communicate in the written word and to polish their writing. You'll need to be the judge of whether this comes early or late in the year. One transitional step is in moving from a tendency to ramble in a "stream of consciousness" style of writing to a tighter piece, staying focused on the stated topic. Here's how you might achieve this focus:

Tell your students, "I'm going to show you several groups of words, and I want you to figure out which word doesn't belong in each group." Show them lists such as:

1	2	3	4	5
rose	spider	run	book	flounder
daisy	ladybug	give	print	perch
petunia	grasshopper	ocean	newspaper	fry
thorn	mosquito	roll	letter	bass
iris	cricket	catch	magazine	trout

The answers are (unless another category is proven by the students):

category 1: flowers; word: **thorn**

category 2: insects; word: **spider**

category 3: verbs/action words; word: **ocean**

category 4: printed materials; word: **print**

category 5: fish; word: **fry**

Explain to students, "Writing is done in categories or groupings, too, and sentences need to fit within these categories."

Give students another category, such as:

Orcas

They often travel in groups called pods.

Guppies are easy fish to raise.

There has never been a report of a human attack by orcas.

They are called killer whales because they attack and kill other whales.

Orcas can live to be 35 years old.

Information on orcas from *Whales and Dolphins: What They Have in Common* by Elizabeth Tayntor Gowell (Franklin Watts, Inc., 2000).

Writing Mini-Lessons for Third Grade: The Four-Blocks® Model

"Let's identify the sentence that doesn't fit. Although it may be related in some way, it strays from the main focus of orcas." Of course, the sentence on guppies relates, but doesn't fit closely in this group of sentences.

If time remains, you might turn this example into a nice paragraph, omitting the sentence that didn't fit.

Remind students, "As you write today, pay close attention to whether all of your sentences stay focused on the topic."

Add to the Editor's Checklist:

5.   I have stayed focused on the topic.

Other Ideas for Staying Focused

- Choosing a title by using the "Goldilocks Rule." Teach students that the title they use for writing should help their reader(s) predict what they'll be reading. Titles may also help students self-check their writing to stay on topic and not include irrelevant information. They won't want to use a title that's smaller than what they're writing about, nor one that's larger than what they'll address in their writing. They'll want to choose a title that's "just right" (Goldilocks Rule) for what they're dealing with. You may want to give them some examples of titles that are too big, too small, and just right.

  For someone who wants to write about pet care for a cat:
  - Cats (too big)
  - Feeding a Cat (too small)
  - Caring for a Cat (just right)

  For someone who wants to write about safety rules related to bicycles:
  - Bicycles (too big)
  - Making a Right Turn on a Bike (too small)
  - Bicycle Safety (just right)

  The above lesson may be easier to do when writing nonfiction, as these topics are often easier to pinpoint. The topic should be the main thing you're telling about in the fewest number of words possible, usually just one or two words. (Later you'll branch out into the use of creative titles and topics that may be longer.)

- As you model your writing for students, read back through the piece and ask sentence-by-sentence, "Is this sentence related to the topic?" If it's questionable, consider striking the sentence. Ask yourself aloud, "What happens if this sentence is removed? Does the meaning change?" If no change is noted, then perhaps the sentence is irrelevant. On several occasions, after students have had adequate time to write, ask them to stop a few minutes early. Encourage them to read back through their papers and to ask themselves those same questions about each sentence.

Mini-Lesson Focus: Spelling by Stretching and Circling

Students often develop some hang-ups about writing. One of the most prevalent ones involves spelling. Often students don't want to write beyond the point of a word that they don't know how to spell. Their solutions are usually one of two: ask the teacher to spell it for them, or look it up in the dictionary. Neither of these options offers a good solution. If you have to stop and spell for every student who can't spell a word, your time will be totally consumed. (There once was a frustrated teacher who wore a sign around her neck that said, "I am not a dictionary!") Also, rough draft writing is not the time to consult with a dictionary, and students need to know that. So, what will we teach them as the very best solution? This is an easy one!

For this lesson, you'll model writing for the students, using any subject. This is a good opportunity for sharing something about yourself—family, pets, hobbies, traditions, and memories of your childhood. Plan your writing so that there will be several words with spellings that might be unfamiliar to many third-grade students.

When you reach the point in your writing where the strategic words are (those that you've determined might be difficult for your students to spell), tell them, "When I was your age, I might not have known how to spell this word. When you're doing your rough draft writing, I really don't want you to worry so much about correctness. I want you to get your thoughts on paper. Later, if you consider that piece for publishing, then we'll fix the spelling at that point. But, I do want you to make your best effort at writing the word well enough that you'll be able to remember what it was when you read it back. So, what I'll do to this word is stretch out the sounds that I hear in the word and put down those sounds on paper." (Excellent might become **eggsellant**, brilliant might become **breelyant**, etc.)

Continue by giving the students an additional aid to help them, "After I stretch out the sounds and write the word, I'll circle it. That way I'll remember to check it later if I work on this piece again." (You won't believe how much circling misspelled words will help some students, especially those who are hung-up on correctness. The circling seems to give them permission to continue and not to feel guilty!)

What I Learned as a Girl Scout

When I was 8 years old, I was a Girl Scout. Looking back now as an adult, I reillize that I learned so many things in Girl Scouts that have been useful to me throughout my life. We all learned to sew basic stiches—handy now for mending socks, sewing on buttons, and making clothes for my children. We learned to grow and care for flowers and vegietables which is why I have a yard that I'm proud of today. We even learned some sirvivil skills from camping in the woods together. That was the part I loved best about Girl Scouts. Camping taught me to reli on my instinks to solve problems and to love nature. Most of all I think that Girl Scouting taught me to respect others and myself, which has made me a better mother, wife, teacher, and citesen.

Note: If you wish to begin teaching students to use proofreading marks in third grade, you can model circling the misspelled word and writing "sp" above the circle.

You may need to remind your students that stretching and circling does **not** apply to Word Wall Words! Those should be spelled correctly all of the time—even in rough draft writing!

Be sure to add this item to your Editor's Checklist!

Add to the Editor's Checklist:

     6.   I have circled words that may be misspelled.

Other Ideas for Teaching Students to Make Approximations in Their Spelling

- Model a piece of writing for students where there is no attempt at true approximations of spellings and other conventions. You might do this as a "live" model or you might have a transparency prepared ahead. In this writing, don't use good rules of spacing; don't use correct punctuation (or don't use punctuation at all); don't take the time to really "stretch out" the sounds in words that are unfamiliar; and don't capitalize words that need to be. Then, have the students help you read it back. This exercise should let them know that rough draft writing is for the purpose of getting ideas on paper and that mistakes are certainly allowed; however, too many mistakes may make writing too difficult to read back. When there is no consistent attempt to use conventions (grammar, spelling, punctuation, capitalization), then the errors can either be too distracting to the reader for understanding to take place, or too much trouble to navigate.

- The "Circle Game": Either create a piece of writing of your own or use an old piece of student writing (not from this year's class and not using any names or details that would identify the student). Be sure that the writing has many misspellings. Display the writing on the overhead projector so that students can read along with you. Tell them that they are all to become editors as you read the paper together. When you come to a word that they feel is misspelled, they should shout, "Circle!" That means that you should stop and circle the word so that it's identified as a "likely misspelled" word. You can make this competitive by letting different small groups help with individual sentences. If anyone in the group shouts "Circle!" and other groups challenge the word and the word isn't misspelled, the group loses a point. If they complete the sentence correctly, the group gets a point.

- Here is an additional idea for a mini-lesson to follow-up on the "Circle Game." After the class has decided which words need to be circled in the piece of writing, ask them if the "stretching" that was done is adequate. Are the sounds in the word all represented? If not, have them help you to add letters—even if they're not correct for the spelling—that will help the reader read the composition.

- Write a short piece of writing or, again, use a piece written by a student who will not be identified. The piece of writing should have a number of spelling errors in it. Make multiple copies of the piece, enough for each student or for every two to three students since all students will need to be able to see the paper. Pass out the piece of writing during the mini-lesson time.

Mini-Lesson Focus: Using the Classroom Environment as a Resource

Four-Blocks classrooms provide print-rich environments for students—Word Walls with words under each letter of the alphabet, cluster charts of words that are related by themes or concepts, much student-created work, and other displays. Teachers must learn to be selective with what and how much is displayed in the classroom. Too much in the environment may tend to overwhelm students to the point that nothing is noticed. (Can't see the forest for the trees!) Teachers must model exactly how the resources chosen for the environment can be useful in reading and writing. It's the transfer or use in "real" writing and reading that's critical!

When words are placed on the Word Wall, tell students, "My expectation is that you'll always use those words correctly—even in your rough draft writing." Then, show the students how the words can become a part of their daily writing.

Plan to model a piece of writing that allows you to use several different words that are displayed on the Word Wall. As you are writing, pause before each of the Word Wall words (those highlighted in the short piece below), and say, "Oh, I know I can spell this word correctly since it's on the Word Wall," as you look at the wall and spell the word correctly in your model writing.

Here It Comes!

There are certain symptoms I've learned to notice that signal that I'm getting a much dreaded cold. First, I get very tired, especially at times during the day when I'm not usually tired. For example, I usually have a lot of energy in the late afternoon, except when a cold is coming on. Another symptom is that I get a scratchy throat. I keep swallowing and coughing which makes getting any rest impossible. The last symptom is that my eyes look different as I'm getting a cold. I look like I've been watching a sad movie with red, puffy, watery eyes. There's not a lot that I can do when I realize that a terrible cold is coming. I just get a box of tissues, some throat lozenges, and prepare to be miserable!

On some occasions, rather than merely looking at the Word Wall and copying the word correctly, give a verbal clue to students as you think aloud about the word that's displayed on the Word Wall. For example, a clue for the word **when** in the passage above might be, "Oh, it's under the **w**'s and relates to **time**." Hopefully, this will encourage students to search the wall with you to guess what you're going to write. It's like giving them a riddle to solve!

With words on the Word Wall or with charts that display word families or spelling patterns, model the use of these patterns as you write. When you come to a word that has the same sound pattern as another word that is displayed like **paste** and **haste** or **fright** and **light**, just tell students, "Oh, **fright** sounds like **light**, so I'll write it with that spelling pattern."

For example, the teacher who writes, "I ought to know better," comes to the word **ought** and thinks aloud, "The word **thought** is on our Word Wall and **ought** rhymes with that word. I'll use **thought** to help me spell this word. Then, she writes **ought** and says, "Yes, that looks right!"

Writing Mini-Lessons for Third Grade: The Four-Blocks® Model

She might also write, "We will go, although it's cold outside." When she comes to the word **although**, she might say, "Now, **although** has the same sound as the word **slow**. I'm going to spell it **a-l-t-h-o-w** for now." Then, after writing **althow**, the teacher says, "That really doesn't look right, so I'll circle it and leave it that way for now. I'll be able to read this back clearly, and I can change it later if I have time to look it up in the dictionary."

You must teach students that just because a word sounds like another word doesn't necessarily mean that it's spelled the same way. You must reassure the students that you will accept misspellings in their rough drafts for words other than Word Wall words. Let them know that you **do** expect them to stretch out the sounds they hear and circle words they may have misspelled.

Other Ideas for Using the Classroom Environment as a Resource

- Try the "Sounds Like" game when modeling writing for students to make them more aware of how we rely on patterns when we want to write a word we don't know. Inform students that as you write that day, you're going to stop on certain words you're writing and say, "Sounds like . . . ." When you say that, the students should quickly look at the Word Wall or other pattern charts in the room and find a word that sounds like the word you've just written. The word may or may not be spelled using the same rime or spelling pattern. After saying, "Sounds like . . . ," you'll count aloud slowly to five. If the class finds the sound-alike word, the class gets a point, but if they don't, then you get a point.

- Allow students to edit your work for Word Wall words that might be misspelled. Tell them you'll make some occasional errors to try to keep them on their toes. You may want to offer some additional incentive for them to watch carefully for Word Wall words. One idea is to purchase a package of large, multicolored, plastic chain links. Each time the students catch you misspelling a Word Wall word, add a link to the chain. Suspend the links in an area of the room. When the links touch down to a specified length (when they touch the floor, perhaps), there may be some special treat—extra recess time, extra self-selected reading time, popcorn to eat during the Self-Selected Reading Block, etc. This will surely cause students to view the Word Wall constantly.

- Plan a composition that you'll write for students and include a number of words from the Word Wall. Let students know that as you write, you'll pause before writing each Word Wall word and will give them a chance to help you spell the word. You can either pause without giving any clues and see if they're reading along with you and anticipating what to write. Or, you may give them a clue, like the letter the word starts with or a clue related to the meaning or use of the word.

- In a composition you've prepared for students, misspell a number of Word Wall words and/or pattern words. Copy the composition for students and give them a few minutes to edit it. Use your mini-lesson time to review as a whole group the work that the students did as editors. Editing is a skill they'll need to do to self-edit their own work and to peer-edit with their classmates.

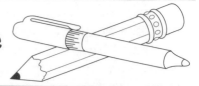

Mini-Lesson Focus: Editing with an Editor's Checklist

There comes a time during the writing process that children must clean up their writing for spelling, mechanics, and grammar errors. This quick edit will make it easier for the reader to read back the writing. The writing will not be clear of all errors. If the piece is to be published, additional revising and editing will be needed. Each Editor's Checklist is introduced, taught, and displayed, then the children are accountable for checking for the correct use of these skills in their rough draft writing.

A typical Editor's Checklist should be clear and concise, and should communicate what skills should be used correctly. There are a variety of ways to display the checklist. The list can be computer-generated, written on sentence strips, written on a poster with each point written in a different color of marker, etc. Teachers should add the items one at a time as they are introduced or reviewed with the class. Often they are numbered so that the students may record the number in the top right corner of their writing as they edit.

The checklist should be used as children edit by themselves, with a peer, with the teacher, or with a group. The teacher models using the checklist daily as model lessons are written.

Here is an example of an Editor's Checklist after the teacher has introduced and taught each item through individual mini-lessons early in the year:

Editor's Checklist

1. I have included my name and the date.
2. I have used capital letters where appropriate.
3. I have used correct ending punctuation.
4. I have used sentences that express complete thoughts.
5. I have stayed focused on the topic.
6. I have circled words that may be misspelled.

Begin by thinking aloud, "I just can't remember everything to check for in my writing unless I write it down. Your teacher last year might have had a poster on the wall with a list of things to remember. We have been creating the checklist that is displayed in our room this year! We will continue to add to this list as we have mini-lessons on important things to remember when we write. As you watch me write each day, I will often refer to the checklist to be sure my writing is easy to read back and is as free of errors as possible."

Now, choose a piece of writing with a variety of errors to use as a model of how to use the Editor's Checklist.

Suzanne
October 22, 2002

The School Playground

Our school playground is packed with equipmet to play on We all run when the bel rings to play on our favorit piece. the cold wind blows. My friend, mary, and i like to play on the swings. Very high. we sometimes have to share them with another class. We look forward to recess every day.

As you read through the writing example, ask the class to assist you in editing the writing by referring to each item on the checklist.

- Name and date are present.

- Capitalize **The**, **Mary**, **I**, and **We**.

- Add a period at the end of the first sentence.

- The words **_very high_** do not make a complete sentence. Change this to: **When we go very high in the air, it tickles our tummies.**

- Remove the sentence that is not focused on the topic: **The cold wind blows**.

- Circle the misspelled words: **equipmet** (equipment), **bel** (bell), and **favorit** (favorite).

Other Ideas for Editing with an Editor's Checklist

- Develop a form for the children to use when they edit by themselves, with a partner, or with you.

- Select a piece of third-grade writing from a previous class to use on the overhead. Allow the students to assist you in using the Editor's Checklist to perform a quick edit.

- As you model writing, demonstrate the use of the Editor's Checklist. Students enjoy using different colors of markers to mark errors.

- Print the Editor's Checklist on a bookmark so the students are reminded in all classes or at home of the basic quick edit skills.

Mini-Lesson Focus: Encouraging Growth in the Writing Process

One day you'll look around the classroom during the Writing Block and find yourself saying, "Gosh! They're all busy with their writing today!" You'll realize, too, that what you've been reading lately of your students' writing, on the whole, shows growth. Now, you'll know it's time to take a giant step forward!

Begin by telling the class, "Now, we're changing the writing steps a little. Your writing is looking pretty good, and I think you're about ready to become published authors!

"You'll need to write three good pieces, beginning from today, and then we'll have a conference together. In our conference, we'll select one piece among those that you've written that we'll work on to publish." (You must define the number of pieces that you feel is appropriate for your students' cycle of writing. Usually anywhere from 3-5 pieces is a good number.)

For each of these pieces, they should continue in the regular cycle:

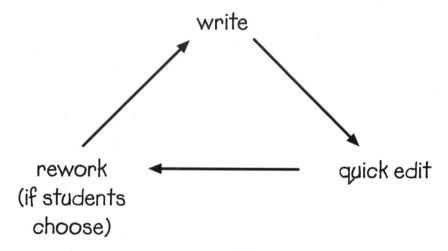

Tell your students, "When we have our conference, this will be our chance to work together to polish and edit your writing. All of your favorite authors have editors, too! Now you'll have your own personal editor—me!" Reassure your students that your time together will help them to become even better writers.

Explain to your students how they will publish their writing once they have been through the process with you. After you've worked together, they'll rewrite the piece they've selected and will then be ready to publish it in some way.

Now the writing process is:

For all 3–5 pieces:

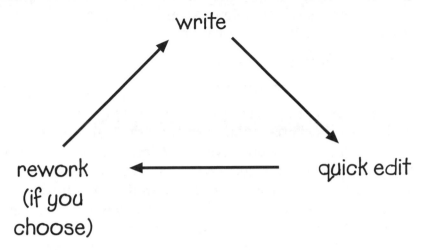

For the one piece that is chosen from the 3–5 pieces:

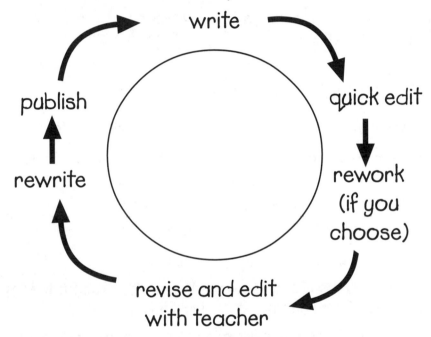

Other Ideas for Encouraging Growth in the Writing Process

- You should also model this new cycle of writing for your students. After you've written 3–5 good pieces, choose one of those pieces for publication. Pinpoint something about the piece you select that you can work to revise (further develop an idea, remove irrelevant information, write a better lead sentence, add more sensory details, etc.). Do this work in front of the students as you think aloud and make the decisions that writers make about their work. After you've revised, do a thorough edit of the paper, perhaps asking students' opinions about your work. Teachers can make books, too, and if that's the way the students will publish, you should do that. (Maybe you can convince other teachers to publish stories, too, and your collected works can be displayed in some prominent place—the library, the hallway, etc.—so that all students will see that teachers value writing and publishing!)

Mini-Lesson Focus: Painting a Picture with Descriptive Words

Writing will have much more impact and will grab the reader's interest if students learn to show and not just tell in their writing. When students use descriptive images to express their ideas or to describe something, the writing shows more development.

This mini-lesson can be taught over a two-day period.

___

Think aloud: "When I write a description, I always want to show what I am talking about and not just tell about it. I think I will write this simple sentence. 'The principal was surprised.' I wonder if I can change some of the words to show an action of surprise? I have to think about some events when the principal was surprised. I remember how surprised Mrs. Gregory was when Matt won the school writing contest. We were all so excited! The day she received a letter full of money for books for our book drive was also a thrill! Then, a not-so-good surprise came when she discovered a student had faked sickness to stay home for the day. Now, I can rewrite the simple sentence to show surprise. Let's see if this will work. 'As dollar bills spilled out of the envelope, the principal leaped with surprise!' Now this is writing that shows!"

A day or two before the writing mini-lesson, read aloud *Spider the Horrible Cat* by Nanette Newman. During the Writing Block, remind the students of this descriptive story and list characteristics that Spider possessed.

unusual, wriggly, snarly, mean, nasty, selfish

Next, model writing a descriptive paragraph about Spider that paints a picture for the reader:

> Spider was quite a cat! When he was hungry, nothing was safe in his house. He was wriggly and snarly as he rubbed against the velvet chair cushion. Sometimes, he would tear through the house leaping over the new blue sofa and knocking over the expensive crystal vase. Until Spider heard the wh-r-r-r of the electric can opener, he was a nasty cat!

Discuss how descriptive word choices such as **wriggly**, **snarly**, **rubbed**, **tear**, **wh-r-r-r**, and **nasty** help the reader form an image from showing and not just telling.

Ask the students to choose a character from a piece of literature they've read or that has been read aloud. Brainstorm descriptive character traits that include action and appearance, and then write a descriptive paragraph that paints a picture for the reader.

Other Ideas for Painting a Picture with Descriptive Words

- Show students a picture painted by a famous artist. Model making a list of descriptive words or phrases that describe the picture and then writing a paragraph using as many words from the list as possible.

- Find examples in literature of descriptive words that form vivid images. Model writing these words or phrases by making a list that can be posted in the room and added to when you find new ideas.

    Here are two examples:

    The Bootmaker and the Elves by Susan Lowell (Orchard Books, 1997)

    > "as skinny as a snake on stilts"

    > "feathered out in fancy duds"

    > "high-heeled, knee-high, needle-nosed working boots"

    Agatha's Feather Bed by Carmen Deedy (Peachtree Publishers, 1994)

    > "mattress was lumpy and bumpy"

    > "sleeping on coal lumps and cherry pits"

    > "hushed whispers and the pitter patter of little feet"

- Select a place or a person studied in the social studies curriculum. Model writing to show what appearances or actions describe the place or person. Ask the students to choose from a list of people or places to write about. By drawing or visualizing before writing, a more vivid word choice will result.

- Show students how to interview someone by asking questions and then writing a paragraph about that person to make them seem like the most interesting person in the class. Choose describing words that paint a picture for the reader.

Mini-Lesson Focus: Using Sensory Details

When you describe with sensory details, you give the reader a unique and more complete picture. This description may include information on sound, feeling, smell, taste, and/or sight. Similes and metaphors are often used in this type of description. After hearing numerous descriptive passages from books, articles, etc., third-graders are ready to include sensory details in their writing.

Brainstorm sensory words relating to each of the five senses. Head five columns with the words Hearing, Seeing, Tasting, Touching, and Smelling. List sensory words under each of the senses. Write a paragraph modeling how to use sensory words in your writing.

Tell your students, "Since we have been reading many stories full of sensory words, I thought it would be interesting to try to add some of these types of words to our own writing. Using describing words will make our writing come to life! Our words will be so much more interesting to read and to picture. I don't think I have ever told you about the vegetable garden that my daddy always had in the summertime. I can think of some really great describing words to use. I am going to brainstorm different describing words and add them to a sensory word chart, then I can write a paragraph using some of these words."

Hearing	Seeing	Tasting	Touching	Smelling
noisy	glaring	delicious	sticky	pungent
quiet	peaceful	sour	sharp	musty
chatter	shimmering	salty	smooth	aromatic
muffled	glossy	flavorful	slick	herbal
muted	faded	fresh	rough	pleasant

Our Vegetable Garden

My daddy loved to plant vegetables in the garden behind his two-story house. These vegetables grew to be large, colorful, and delicious! On a quiet, peaceful morning, we could hear him digging away at the weeds with a sharp, slick hoe. He would gather the ripest vegetables to add to the fresh, flavorful lunch my mother would prepare. Pleasant smells would float through the house as the smooth tomatoes cooked in a stew. Crunchy carrots, pungent peppers, and aromatic spices would make the stew smell even more wonderful. My daddy was so proud that he had grown so much of our food in his abundant vegetable garden.

Give students a list of nouns. Model adding sensory details to describe each noun.

Provide students a form such as the one above. Have them choose 3–5 nouns to describe with sensory details and then to write about in descriptive sentences.

Noun	Sensory Details
bear	grizzly, furry, woodsy, grumpy
snowflakes	white, feathery, cold, silent
strawberry	juicy, red, sweet, bumpy, squishy

Then, write:

The juicy, red strawberry tasted so sweet. As I bit into this tasty fruit, I could hear a squishy sound.

Allow students time to share with the whole group or with a partner. As the sentences are read aloud, ask the class to use their senses to understand the sentences.

After this type of practice, the students should be ready to add good describing words to their own writing.

Other Ideas for Using Sensory Details

• Show an overhead of a piece of fine art. Divide the class into five groups. Set the timer for five minutes. Ask the groups to generate as many sensory details about the piece in this amount of time. Ask the leader of each group to share their list with the class.

• Select a classroom object or object from home to observe with the senses. This object could be food (a piece of fruit), an article of clothing (shoe), toy, etc. Record descriptive words about the object.

• Write descriptions and have students guess the object.

For example:

It is slender and hard. It is bright yellow. The tip is made of a softer material that smells musky.

(Answer: a pencil)

• Select a fictional character. Picture each of the five senses. Write a paragraph with sensory details describing the character. Here are some examples:

  Harry Potter
  Owen (from the Kevin Henkes's book)
  Stuart Little

Mini-Lesson Focus: Working at the Beginning of a Story (Setting and Character)

Third-graders are becoming more proficient at writing personal and imaginative narratives. Stories have been a major part of their lives. Many of the TV programs and selections used as read-alouds revolve around this text structure. The children can now be responsible for writing organized narratives that include a beginning, middle, and an end. This lesson will focus on the characters and setting to be introduced in the beginning of the story. The setting includes sentences that explain where and when the story takes place. When writing to a test prompt, many third-graders ramble through time, writing narratives with no clear time focus.

Choose 2–3 examples of simple books that clearly show the elements of character, place, and time in a story. Kevin Henkes's books serve as excellent models (*Owen, Chrysanthemum,* or *Julius, Baby of the World*). Read the descriptions of the characters and the setting (place and time focus). Use the book examples to complete a chart either on the overhead or chart paper. Model writing the beginning of a story choosing a character, place, and time.

Think aloud, then write: "Today, I want to tell you about my grandfather and his flower garden. I want to be sure to include whom the story is about, and where and when it takes place."

> My grandfather, Andrew Rowell, grew the most beautiful dahlias in his flower garden. Every summer I would visit him. I would always find my grandfather working in his garden.

Ask the children to assist in identifying the character, place, and time of the story. Use three different colors of markers. Underline each part in a different color.

After turning off the overhead, ask the children to write, telling you the character, place, and time of their stories. With three colored pencils, ask them to underline the three parts of their stories.

As children share their writing with a partner, they reinforce setting organization.

Note: Save the transparency of this story setting to use in a series of lessons to follow.

Other Ideas for Working at the Beginning of a Story (Setting and Character)

• Third-graders are ready to group or cluster ideas. They can now see how to put ideas together to create a clear character and setting. Model how to brainstorm ideas in the following categories. Share people, places, and times that could be written about. An overhead projector and transparency will assist the children in focusing on the writing.

People (Who)	Places (Where)	Times (When)
mom	my bedroom	one morning
dad	kitchen	one afternoon
brother	porch	one night
sister	church	at lunch
friends	zoo	in the spring
uncle	backyard	in the summer
aunt	state fair	in the fall
cousin	museum	in the winter
grandmother	barn	at 2:00 p.m.
grandfather	school	last year

Give the children a blank form and ask them to brainstorm lists of people, places, and times that could be the settings of their stories. Allow partners to share their lists. Then, ask 2–3 children to read their lists to the class. Encourage the children to add others' ideas to their own personal lists.

• When third-graders write personal narratives, they often focus on an event or experience such as a special birthday, a visit with grandparents, an exciting summer vacation, etc. Use **who, where,** and **when** questions to stimulate the memories that will form the beginning of a story.

• Tell the students to write characters, places, and times on index cards. Shuffle each set of cards. Students will find it amusing as they draw one card from each set to create a new character and setting for a story.

Mini-Lesson Focus: Working in the Middle of a Story (Adding Details)

The next lesson in this series of writing beginnings, middles, and endings of stories will focus on what to do in the middle. It makes sense to continue with the story that was started in the first lesson on character and setting and demonstrate how to add on more information.

Start by reminding the children about the story you started: "Remember the story I started writing that was about my grandfather and his flower garden? We have a good beginning, but I have much more I want to tell you about this topic! These details will make up the middle of my story. I think that it will be a good idea to work on the middle of the story today. I will start by rereading the beginning. Now, you probably have some questions, because I didn't tell you very much. What else would you like to know?"

Read the story beginning to the class. Generate questions they may have and begin to add supporting details. Underline the details that were added, making sure that each detail supports the topic.

> My grandfather, Andrew Rowell, grew the most beautiful dahlias in his flower garden. Every summer I would visit him. I would always find my grandfather working in his garden. <u>The dahlias were so tall that I could not see my grandfather. Deep purple, bronze, maroon, and yellow flowers would surround him.</u>

Tell the students to add supporting details to the piece of writing that was crafted for the Working at the Beginning of a Story mini-lesson (page 44).

Writing Mini-Lessons for Third Grade: The Four-Blocks® Model

Other Ideas for Working in the Middle of a Story (Adding Details)

- Continue to add to the chart started in the mini-lesson, Working at the Beginning of a Story (pages 44–45). These memories become the supporting details. As the students write their narratives from the chart, remind them that it should not read like a list. Metaphors and similes could be used to make the writing more interesting.

Who?	
Where?	
When?	
What do I remember?	
Event 1	
Event 2	
Event 3	
Event 4	
Event 5	
Event 6	

- Supporting details need to be written in sequential order. An adequate number is required so that the narrative seems complete. An activity to reinforce this concept would be to list details in order on a transparency. Cut the details apart and then mix them up as they are placed on the overhead. To rearrange the details in the correct order will require the children to think logically.

- Partners can read their personal narratives to each other. The listening partner will pay particular attention to the supporting details by making a tally mark each time he hears one. Students will then share their numbers with the group.

Mini-Lesson Focus: Working at the End of a Story

This lesson is the third in a series about writing stories with beginnings, middles, and endings. Students need to see that the story is not complete without an ending.

Tell the students, "Today I think I will add an ending to the story I started about my grandfather and his flower garden. This ending will make my story complete."

Continue modeling by using the story written for the beginning and the middle mini-lessons. Review with the class the series of mini-lessons on beginnings and middles of stories. Continue with the same story modeled in these previous lessons. Explain that the story is not complete, and that today's lesson will focus on adding an ending.

> My grandfather, Andrew Rowell, grew the most beautiful dahlias in his flower garden. Every summer I would visit him. I would always find my grandfather working in his garden. The dahlias were so tall <u>that I could only see the tip of his wide-brimmed hat</u> that shaded his face. Deep purple, bronze, maroon, and yellow flowers surrounded him.

Now, think aloud different ways in which the story could end:

"I could end the story by telling about the beautiful flower arrangements that were made with the flowers. Or, I could write about how my grandfather would cut some of the dahlias for me to take home. I think I would like to end my story telling you about getting to take the flowers home."

Continue by adding the following ending on the overhead to the story that was previously started.

> The flowers were so beautiful. It was a thrill to see my grandfather cut them and then ask if I would like to take flowers home. I was always happy to take the flowers with me. Seeing the dahlias in my own home reminded me of my grandfather and his beautiful flower garden.

Other Ideas for Working at the End of a Story

• Read several narrative stories such as *Tough Boris* by Mem Fox, *More Than Anything Else* by Marie Bradby, etc. Before reaching the conclusion, stop reading. Close the book as if you were finished. The children will become frustrated when they think they will not hear the ending. Lead them to see how their own narrative stories are incomplete without endings.

• During read-aloud time, examine the different ways authors end their stories. Give students an opportunity to write down on a piece of paper different endings from books in the classroom or school library. This list of endings can be added to the students' writing folders or notebooks. As they revise endings to their own stories, this list can be a resource.

• Use examples of third-grade student writing on the overhead. Cover the ending and ask the class to come up with possible ways the narrative could be concluded. Uncover the endings and determine which way was closest to the original ending.

Mini-Lesson Focus: Sequencing

Many times it is necessary to write out an explanation of how to do something or to write a series of events in order. Planning this writing activity around authentic events in a third-grader's world will motivate the student to attack this assignment with gusto! This lesson may need to be taught over a two-day period.

Day One

Begin by reminding the class, "Remember that we have been reading an article about family traditions, and we all discussed interesting traditions in our own families. This week we will participate in a creative art activity that can be a new tradition for your family. The activity will be successful and fun if everyone follows the directions in a sequential order."

Model writing directions in paragraph form for how to complete the craft activity.

Tell your students, "Today, I will write a paragraph where the purpose is not to describe or to persuade, but instructs you on how to do a craft activity. Be sure to observe the many sequence words used to communicate order."

A Family Tradition

It is easy and fun to make a memory box for your family. This box will be a place to keep items that remind you of special memories. You will need a shoe box, aluminum foil, dried pasta shapes, glue, a pencil, and colored markers. Before you begin, tear off enough aluminum foil to cover the lid and the bottom of the shoe box. First, cover the two box pieces with the foil. Glue may be needed to keep the foil in place. Next, use a pencil to write the words "Memory Box" on top of the lid. Then, lay the pasta pieces on the pencil lines and glue them down, one at a time. While the glue dries on the lid, glue pasta pieces around the sides of the box to create interesting designs. Last, use colored markers to decorate the pasta shapes. You now have a beautiful memory box and a new family tradition!

Reread the paragraph and draw a line under each sequence word or phrase (**Before you begin**, **First**, **Next**, **Then**, and **Last**). List these words on a separate chart to display in the room.

Day Two

After completing the art activity, tell the students to write a paragraph telling someone how to make this memory box. Remind them of the many sequence words that may be used. Instruct them to underline these words. Add any new sequence words to the classroom chart.

Other Ideas for Sequencing

- Other topics can be used to teach students to write in sequence. For example, have them provide an explanation for:

> How to Make a Pizza
>
> How to Plant a Flower
>
> How to Clean Your Room (Make a Bed)
>
> How to Wash Dishes

- Model for the students how to write out directions for playing a board game. Demonstrate how important it is for a sequence to be correct so the game can be played by the rules. Place familiar games in a game area of the classroom. Then, have the students write out the directions on how to play the games. Allow the students to play the game by following a classmate's directions.

- You could also model how to write a series of events in order. Phrases that are appropriate for use could be: *at first, in the beginning, recently, starting off, after, after a while, later, at the same time, the next thing, also, in addition to, at last,* and *finally.* Examples of topics for writing a series of events:

> My Trip to the Zoo
>
> Getting Ready for School
>
> Shopping for Groceries

- Construct a form to fill in with sequence words. Model completing this form from writing done the day before. Ask the students to fill in the form with sequence words they have used in their writing. This form can be kept in the writing folder and added to during the year.

My Own Sequence Words
1.
2.
3.
4.
5.
6.
7.
8.
9.
10.

Mini-Lesson Focus: Developing Characters

Whether students are writing about characters created in their imaginations or about people they know well, they must learn how to tell about those characters in their writing so that readers can easily picture them. Usually students tend to describe only the physical attributes of the character(s) and stop there. Tell them that there are many ways that they can let readers know what characters are like—inside and out!

For this lesson, you'll need to read a story aloud that has a character who has been developed by the author in a number of different ways—through actions, through what the character says, or through what others say about the character. You might present the story as your read-aloud in the Self-Selected Reading Block, use a story from the Guided Reading Block, or use a well-known character from a fairy or folk tale. Cinderella is a good character to start with.

Say to students, "Let's describe the character by telling what the character looked like." Start a chart and make **Physical Description** or **What does the character look like?** the first column heading.

After listing the physical attributes, ask the students, "Are there other things you know about the character besides what the character looks like?" Hopefully, the students will say that they know other things.

Tell them and show them that there are a number of ways that writers typically tell readers what their characters are like. Add these headings to your chart:

What does the character do?
What does the character say or think?
What do others say or think about the character?

Here's a chart based on a class discussion about Cinderella:

Things We Know about the Character

What does the character look like?	What does the character do?	What does the character say or think?	What do others say or think about the character?
Blonde hair "Barbie-like" Dirty in beginning Beautiful when Fairy Godmother helps her	Continues to do chores well Worries about disobeying Disobeys stepmother but for a good reason Kind to stepmother and stepsisters after she marries the Prince	Says that she is not treated fairly but is tolerant Makes decision to go to ball and disobeys (with good reason)	Animals speak kindly about her Fairy Godmother says she is kind Stepmother and stepsisters say she is a good person even in their complaints Prince says she is beautiful and sweet

Other Ideas for Developing Characters

- In follow-up lessons, ask students to help you decide how many different ways you developed your characters, using the questions in the chart of the main lesson. You may not always need to write down their responses, but reading the questions and asking students to see if they have any evidence that you've used different ways of developing your characters will help them to ask themselves those questions when they write.

- Let students know that characters who are developed in only one way, especially through physical attributes, tend to be "flat" characters. We want "well-rounded" characters! A graphic of flat and well-rounded characters on the wall of your writing center might provide a good reminder.

- When you have completed a story written for students in your modeling time, conclude by asking students to trace their hands on a sheet of paper. Ask them to write your character's name in the center of their handprints. Ask them to read back through your story and to write in each finger something that they have learned about the character. They're not required to have five things, but, hopefully, they'll have evidence of several things they've learned from your piece.

Mini-Lesson Focus: Developing Settings

You want students to develop a sense of appropriate setting for their stories. Setting, in its broadest definition, includes the **where** and the **when** of a story. **Where** might be: Africa, downtown, my room, in the kitchen, in a dream, on a boat, etc. **When** might be: yesterday, 1972, at night, September, winter, after the test, at 10:00 A.M., etc.

You'll want to read several stories over a number of days. Some of the stories might be those read during your read-aloud in the Self-Selected Reading Block; some may be those read during Guided Reading, or some short ones may be read during the Writing Block.

After students have heard each story, take another look at the stories for evidence of when and where the story took place. Model one or two aloud for them, recording evidence of where and when the story took place on a chart for the students.

"In figuring out the setting of *Little Red Riding Hood*, I'm going to look for all of the clues that will tell me when and where the story took place. First, in this book, the illustrator gives me some clues. It's clear that the story is taking place during the daytime. I would have guessed that a little girl would not be walking through the woods at night alone! There are also descriptions of the forest—that it's thick with trees and patches of light showing through in places. The story actually has two settings. Some of the action takes place outside in the forest, and then I have clues that the action moves inside the grandmother's house. Let me read some of the description of her bedroom and kitchen that I can find."

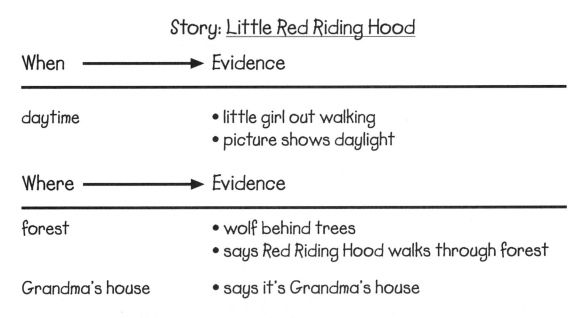

Story: Little Red Riding Hood

When ⟶	Evidence
daytime	• little girl out walking • picture shows daylight

Where ⟶	Evidence
forest	• wolf behind trees • says Red Riding Hood walks through forest
Grandma's house	• says it's Grandma's house

Bring closure to the lesson by leading a discussion about whether the setting was important to the story. Ask, "Could this same story have taken place at some other time or some other place?" Ask students to substantiate their responses, "How did you know that?" For example, "Yes, *Little Red Riding Hood* needed to take place in the forest and at Grandmother's house. Wolves live in the forest, and a wolf is one of the main characters. Also, Grandmother's house gave the wolf a good place to hide to wait for Little Red Riding Hood." Students need to develop a sense of when setting is important to the story. If it is important, the writer will need to spend a little more time developing it. If it is not important, the writer can briefly describe or mention it.

Other Ideas for Developing Settings

- Don't ignore the opportunity to teach about setting as it applies to poems. Teach students to recognize the settings in poems that they read and also to experiment with establishing settings for their own poems. This might be a good time to explore poems that don't rhyme. The beauty of this genre is the conciseness with which ideas are expressed. Be brave and model your own poems!

- Settings can be described through the senses—taste, touch, sight, smell, sound. In your model lesson, brainstorm with children how you can describe settings through senses. The chart below may help you.

Setting	Taste	Touch	Sight	Smell	Sound
the fair	popcorn cotton candy	metal	lights carousel	food animal exhibits	music screams

Use ideas from the chart to write a poem or to establish the setting for a story. You might try writing some poetic riddles about settings, using only the sensory words for clues. Below is a poem, fashioned like a riddle, which hints at a specific setting. What are the clues about **where** and **when**?

Where Am I?

Horses bobbing up and down

Big bright wheels turning round and round

Cotton candy and elephant ears

Screaming voices filled with fears

Much excitement in the cool night air

My favorite times are at the _____!

Mini-Lesson Focus: Developing Plot

Often teachers feel that narratives should be the easiest genre for students to write, especially since students have been exposed to many stories by third grade. However, students at all grades struggle to create narratives. One of the reasons for this is that students often don't have a good sense of what constitutes a story. They may feel that stories are the stuff that movies are made of, and yet, those stories are not at all within their young experiences (probably not within the experiences of most adults either!). Teachers must try hard to convince students that they have stories worthy of writing within their everyday lives.

Day One

Share with students the basic structure of a narrative in the simplest terms possible. "Almost all stories have some basic ingredients, just like most bread has the same basic ingredients. Stories have these ingredients: characters, problems, solutions, and an ending." Write these terms in a chart similar to the one below.

Next, recall with students different, simple stories that fit this traditional framework. You might use fairy tales, common to most students, or stories you've all read in the Guided Reading or Self-Selected Reading Blocks as examples. A sample follows, using *Little Red Riding Hood*, *The Three Little Pigs*, and *Cinderella* (stories that most students would know):

Characters	Problem	Solution	Ending
Grandmother Red Riding Hood Wolf Hunter	RRH wants to deliver cookies to Granny but Wolf wants to eat RRH	Hunter with axe comes to RRH's rescue and saves her from Wolf	Lives happily ever after and RRH learns not to talk to strangers!
three little pigs Big Bad Wolf	Wolf wants to eat three little pigs	Pigs outsmart Wolf as he tries to blow down house of smartest pig	Pigs live happily ever after!
Cinderella two stepsisters stepmother Fairy Godmother Prince	Stepmother and stepsisters try to keep Cinderella from meeting the Prince	Cinderella goes to ball with help of Fairy Godmother and animals; meets Prince	Cinderella marries Prince, is kind to stepmother and stepsisters, and lives happily ever after!

Day Two

Think of a simple story about everyday life, maybe something you've experienced, that fits into the framework you used on the previous day with students. Keeping your story simple and about daily life will help students pick the events in their lives that will make good stories.

Tell the story aloud as you fill in the chart. "I want to tell you about how my neighbor's cat has been adopted by our family. Let me think how my simple story might have the same elements that any story might have." An example of the chart might be:

Characters	Problem	Solution	Ending
me, my husband, my neighbor, the neighbor's cat, Whiskers	neighbors get a new kitten and their cat, Whiskers, moves to our house	make an agreement with neighbors that Whiskers can live with us and they will pay vet bills	Whiskers lives with our family

Day Three

Use the chart from Day Two as a framework to write your story. You can take as many days as necessary to write a good story. Stress often that the best stories are the ones that are within the experience of the writer.

The Adoption of Whiskers

I've never considered myself a cat-lover. Dogs are more my style. So, when Whiskers, our neighbor's calico cat, showed up on our doorstep, I was puzzled about what to do. Day and night she sat at our door and pawed at the glass door to get in.

When the weather turned cold outside, my husband and I were concerned that Whiskers needed some shelter. We really didn't want to let her in, though. So, my husband carried the cat next door to ask if the neighbors were missing their cat. They told him that they had a new kitten and that Whiskers didn't seem to care for him. In fact, they said she had moved out the very day they had gotten the kitten.

After trying many days to coax Whiskers back home without success, we knew we had to come to an agreement with the neighbors. We finally decided that they would pay the vet bills, and we would allow Whiskers to stay with us. I guess this was an adoption. That's how this non-cat-lover became a cat-lover after all!

Other Ideas for Developing a Plot

• Once your students understand the basic formula or structure for narrative development, you will want to carry them a step further. Teach students that often the ending of the story is better if the writer allows feelings to be known in response to what has happened. You may want to retrieve the story you wrote on the Day Three lesson to elaborate a bit on the underlying feelings. For example, in the conclusion of the story about the neighbor's cat moving in, you might write:

Although I really didn't want a cat, I must admit that I was touched by the fact that Whiskers picked us as her new family. It's rare that family members get to do that! I know that we'll be one big, happy family—my husband, my dog, me, and now, our adopted cat, Whiskers!

Mini-Lesson Focus: Using Quotation Marks in Writing

Students at the third-grade level really enjoy experimenting with dialogue in their writing. Occasionally, they'll even admit that they like using all of the "fancy" punctuation marks that go along with writing dialogue. These model lessons will help students understand how to use dialogue effectively to make their characters come to life.

For this lesson, you can use a newspaper cartoon strip (that your students can relate to) in which there are two characters engaged in a simple conversation. (*Peanuts, Garfield, Family Circus,* etc.) The cartoon can have one or more frames. Transfer it onto a transparency. You may want to enlarge the cartoon if your copy machine has enlargement capabilities, so that students can clearly see the words.

Display the cartoon strip on the overhead projector and read through it with the students. Tell the students, "Cartoons can easily show action through the use of pictures and dialogue. I want to show you how to make characters in your stories come to life through the use of dialogue."

Translate the cartoon into dialogue on the remaining portion of the transparency. You may need to add some narration to explain some of the action that isn't included in the words spoken by the characters.

Think aloud as you include punctuation marks that show the exact words the characters are speaking: "I need open quotation marks here to show that this is where the character is beginning to talk. Here I'm putting a comma and closed quotation marks to show that he's through talking, but I still need to make it clear just who's talking. So, I'm going to add 'yelled Joe' since he's shouting this sentence, and then I'll add a period to end this whole sentence." Tell students that, quite often, new paragraphs are started each time a different person speaks.

Read the dialogue along with students once you've written it for them.

Add to the Editor's Checklist:

       7.   I have used quotation marks correctly.

Other Ideas for Using Quotation Marks in Writing

- To have students get a feel for the exact words that will go inside of the quotation marks when people "talk" in their writing, show them how to create simple storyboards. Inside the frames, draw characters with dialogue bubbles of direct words spoken. These can later be changed into written dialogue, much like the main lesson using a cartoon.

- Model dialogue in your own writing where you use the three main ways of punctuating dialogue. Place the speaker before the quotation, in the middle of the quotation, and at the end of the quotation. For example:

  He shouted, "Stop! Come back and help me!"

  "Stop!" he shouted, "Come back and help me!"

  "Stop! Come back and help me!" he shouted.

- Have fun letting students get involved kinesthetically in punctuating dialogue. Either have a piece of dialogue reproduced on a transparency for all to read along with you or use multiple copies of the dialogue that everyone reads along with. Determine a sound for each of the punctuation marks that may be involved in punctuating dialogue, such as: comma = whistle; open quotation = clap and open arms; closed quotation = clap and fold hands; period = snap fingers; question mark = pop with tongue; and exclamation mark = hissing sound.

  As you all read together, everyone makes the sound of the marks as you read. Or, you may wish to appoint a punctuation mark and sound to each cooperative group. One group makes the sound for commas, one for open quotations, etc.

- Study the dialogue in various texts: trade books, basals, news articles, etc. Identify characters speaking the lines by having certain students or cooperative groups stand as their character speaks in the text.

- Try typing an excerpt of text from a story on your computer, omitting the punctuation in the dialogue. Reproduce the excerpt on a transparency for all students to work together, or let students work in partners or cooperative groups. Have students insert appropriate punctuation marks, and then check their answers as a class by inserting the correct marks on a transparency.

Note: Let students experiment with the punctuation marks. The most important marks are the quotation marks that will indicate whether or not students understand the exact words that are being spoken. Try to be lenient with the placement of commas at this point, as they are more difficult and technical for third-graders. Model the use of commas, but know that not all students will be ready to use them appropriately.

Mini-Lesson Focus: Narrowing a Research Topic (Using Webs)

Students at all grade levels struggle with narrowing a topic enough for it to be manageable for them. They try to "eat the whole elephant" when, perhaps, only a bite is necessary! For example, they may try to do a short report on sharks. Where do they begin when volumes upon volumes are written about sharks? Students need direct instruction on how to whittle down their topics so that they stay focused and so that when research is involved they have an easier time pulling together their information. Instruction should focus more on the process or framework for pulling the research together than on the depth or length of the paper produced.

Tell your students, "You'll soon be writing a research paper to learn the process we use to write them. If you've heard that report writing is dull and boring or hard, you should put aside all that you've heard. I'll teach you step-by-step what you should do for a good report and how much you can learn about your topic as you write."

First, you'll need to define some broad category—likely something that you're currently studying about in science, social studies, health, or a related content area. In your model lesson, you'll draw a simple web, putting the succinct broad topic in the middle hub. Color coding your web for visual learners may be helpful. Put this main topic in one color. For example, let's say your class is studying about insects in science. Your web would begin this way:

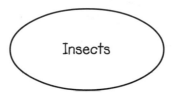

Think aloud: "Now I have the broad category. This topic is way too big to tackle. I'll need to go to the next level. What are the possible types of insects that I might be interested in writing about?" Using another color, put the names of these in the circles that will branch off from **Insects** this way:

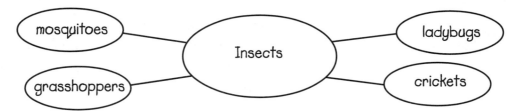

Next you'll decide which of the choices most interests you. Think aloud as you come to this conclusion, such as, "I really don't know much about ladybugs, and I've always thought they were interesting. We also have a number of books in our classroom that will help me gather information about them. I think that will be my choice!"

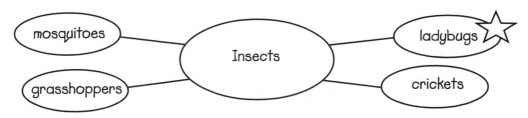

Now brainstorm aloud a number of things that you would really like to know about ladybugs, and, using a third color, write those in the next level of circles branching from the word "ladybugs." You might brainstorm about five different items in this level of the web.

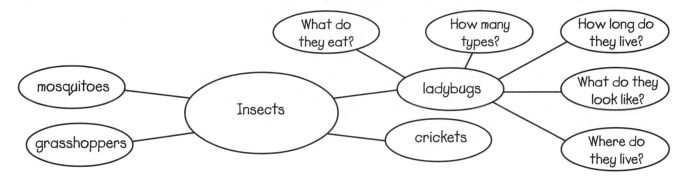

If you have more than three items in the previous level of your web, think aloud as you decide on just three of those items that interest you the most. Put a star or check mark on those three circles.

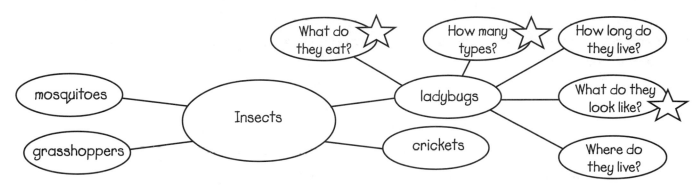

Now, you're off to a great start for research writing! Your students should be able to follow your model to choose a topic and three specific focus questions. There is great value in having them do this exercise several times before moving further into actually gathering information and writing a paper. Remember it's the process that can be so helpful at this stage!

Other Ideas for Narrowing a Research Topic

• The "Goldilocks Rule" to narrowing a topic: Give students examples of topics that are "way too big" to tackle, "way too small" to manage, and those that are "just right." See if they can pick the "just right" ones.

Below are some examples of topics that might fall into each of these categories. Scramble the three topics that relate to the same subject and see if students can fit them correctly into the categories below. (The "just right" answers are in the middle of each of these.)

- Baseball; How Baseball Started; What Year Baseball Started

- Alaska; The Iditarod Sled Race; The Number of Dogs that Pull a Sled

- Dogs; How to Groom a Dog; What Dogs Like to Eat

- Spiders; Poisonous Spiders; The Number of Legs on a Spider

Mini-Lesson Focus: Telling about Similarities and Differences

Third-grade students are beginning to write more and more in the informational mode. Nonfiction text begins to take on a more important role in their reading. So, it makes sense that they will be writing more nonfiction as well. Writing a paragraph that tells similarities and differences requires that a plan be used. Usually the paragraph will begin with a statement that names the items you will tell about. As you elaborate with reasons and details, powerful words should be used. To see how things are similar, we compare them. To see how things are different, we contrast them.

Model writing that tells about similarities and differences. Decide on two items to compare and contrast (for example, bicycles and tricycles).

Tell your students, "Sometimes when I write I need to tell how two things are alike and different. I will need a plan so I can remember all of the reasons to include in my writing. Then, I will need to think of a clear way to begin. I think I will use a chart to brainstorm how bicycles and tricycles are alike and different."

Brainstorm how bicycles and tricycles are alike and different by completing a graphic organizer such as the one below.

Details	Bicycle	Tricycle
two wheels	X	
three wheels		X
goes fast	X	
bright colors	X	X
provides transportation	X	X
handle bars	X	X
pedals	X	X

Write the paragraph.

Bicycles and Tricycles

Have you ever ridden a bicycle or a tricycle? If you have, then you know how they are alike and different. Because they are both things that can be ridden, there are many ways in which they are alike. For example, both bicycles and tricycles provide transportation. In fact, many people use them to ride from one place to another. They both have handlebars and pedals and are painted bright colors. The differences between a bicycle and tricycle have to do with their size and speed. The bicycle with two wheels is larger and can move at a faster speed. In fact, there are many bicycle races, and bicycling is a summer Olympic sport. The tricycle with three wheels is smaller and cannot be ridden as fast. Bicycles and tricycles are both fun to ride.

Ask the students to select two objects in the room and write about their similarities and differences. For example:

- pencil/crayon
- stool/student chair
- chalkboard/magnetic erase board

Other Ideas for Telling about Similarities and Differences

- Read a book and then show a video version of the book. Model how to compare the characters, the settings, and the plots. Set up a graphic organizer to jot down how the characters, the settings, or the plots are alike and different. Write a paragraph comparing and contrasting the two modes. Ask the students to write about how the book and video were alike and different.

- Cut out two pictures from a magazine. Using a Venn Diagram, brainstorm ideas and fill in the circles to show how the pictures are alike and different. Ask the students to compare and contrast the pictures by writing a paragraph about them.

- Choose a fiction book and a nonfiction book about the same subject. Read both of the books for a read-aloud. Discuss with the students how the books are the same and how they are different. After hearing both books read, ask the students to write a paragraph comparing and contrasting them.

For example:

Stellaluna by Janell Cannon (Harcourt, 1993).
Bats by Gail Gibbons (Holiday House, 2000).

Amazing Grace by Mary Hoffman (Scott Foresman, 1991).
The Story of Ruby Bridges by Robert Coles (Scholastic, Inc., 1995).

Mini-Lesson Focus: Using Concrete Examples to Clarify

When writing explanations, it is necessary to include concrete examples so that the reader can form strong mental pictures. Explanations are more effective if the ideas are clarified in this way. Many modeled lessons will assist the students in how to include these examples in their own writing.

Tell your students, "I will show you how writing can be clearer if I use concrete examples. If I write a general statement, such as, 'My dog loves to chew,' then there is not a great deal to picture in my mind's eye when I read this. Now if I add a sentence to this, the picture I have might be clearer. 'My dog loves to chew. Dad had to replace his leather slippers because of Max's antics.' Wow! Now I can really see action in the picture I have in my mind."

Model writing a simple paragraph about whales. Be sure to point out the concrete examples used to clarify statements.

Whales

There are several different types of whales. One of the most interesting types is the Blue Whale. This whale may be the largest animal that ever lived. <u>Pulling this creature out of the ocean is no easy task!</u> The Blue Whale's babies are the largest in the world. <u>These calves can gain up to 200 pounds a day.</u> The Blue Whale takes in huge mouthfuls of water and krill. <u>Using its tongue and cheeks, the krill is trapped inside the whale's mouth.</u> It is no wonder that it grows up to 100 feet long and weighs more than 300,000 pounds.

Information from *Whales and Dolphins: What They Have in Common* by Elizabeth Tayntor Gowell (Franklin Watts, Inc., 2000).

With a marker, go back into the paragraph and underline or circle the concrete examples. Show the students how to complete a topic clarification chart using the information in the paragraph.

Instruct the students to write informational paragraphs about topics they know a lot about. Ask them to include concrete examples.

Topic Statement	Concrete Example
Blue whale is the largest animal	Difficult to pull out of the ocean
Baby blue whales are largest in the world	Gain up to 200 pounds a day
Takes in water and krill	Tongue and cheeks trap krill

On the same day (or Day 2 if necessary), ask the students to complete a topic clarification chart using the information in their paragraphs.

Other Ideas for Using Concrete Examples to Clarify

Give students a piece of writing. (This can be copied from a magazine article, from a nonfiction work, from a student's writing, etc.) Using highlighters, ask students to identify the concrete examples and mark them.

Michael played ball. When March came, he was on the baseball field every day.

The Pilgrims came to North America on ships. Often a different vessel would arrive loaded with these courageous people.

Ask the students to write their own general sentences and add concrete examples.

Identify a character from a story recently read (for example, *Wilfrid Gordon McDonald Partridge* by Mem Fox). Discuss the traits of this character. Help the students write information about the character in a character clarification chart.

Character Clarification Chart for Wilfrid Gordon McDonald Partridge by Mem Fox

Character Trait	How do we know?
kind	Wilfrid visited older people.
sensitive	Wilfrid wanted to help Miss Nancy find her memories.
curious	Wilfrid asked the residents what a "memory" was.

Give students statements of topics from nonfiction pieces. Think about using the science book and give examples from the unit they are currently studying. Ask the students to add concrete examples. Demonstrate this by sharing the following with them on the overhead.

Chameleons have special adaptations to help them capture their prey. Their large eyes can swivel independently to locate prey.

Pythons and boas kill their prey by constriction and suffocation. Victims are wrapped in the snake's powerful coils and squeezed to death.

The polar bears are patient hunters. When they find a seal's breathing hole in the ice, they crouch over it for hours, waiting for the seals to come up for air.

These examples are from *Hunters and Prey* by Beatrice McLeod (Blackbirch Press, Inc., 2000).

Mini-Lesson Focus: Developing Ideas through Questioning

Students in third grade become more discriminating readers and writers. They begin to develop a sense of writing that is done just for writing's sake and writing that is clear and interesting. They realize that they like text that makes them think about things in new and different ways. To help students attain some level of confidence in their own abilities to write interesting pieces and to more fully develop their ideas, try teaching some questioning techniques in your model lessons.

Day One

Read these two short pieces aloud to your students and ask them to vote for the one that they find more interesting:

Selection #1

My Visit to the White House

Last summer I visited the White House in Washington, D.C. We walked through many of the rooms. They were big and pretty. We had a great time and learned a lot about the history of the United States. I hope I'll get to go back and visit again!

Selection #2

My Visit to the White House

Last summer I visited the White House in Washington, D.C. and learned many interesting things about it. Did you know that there are 132 rooms in the White House? The president and his family live on the second floor. The president works in this house, too. Many people think that George Washington lived there, but he never got to move in. He was in charge of building it, but it took eight years. John Adams was the first president to live there. At that time, only six rooms were finished. There were no bathrooms or closets, and the East Room was used to dry laundry! There is a lot to know about this important building. I hope I'll get to go back and visit again!

Information from *The White House* by Tristan Boyer Binns (Heinemann Library, 2001).

Ask students, "Why do you think that the second piece is more interesting than the first? Did you learn some interesting things from the second piece that you didn't know before I read it to you (or before we read it together)?" After their responses, tell students that, "Both fiction and nonfiction are often written to satisfy the questions and curiosity of the reader. Tomorrow we'll take a look at how asking and answering our own questions can help us to develop our ideas on paper."

Day Two

To follow-up on your Day One lesson, begin to write a piece of your own. After choosing the topic, whether fiction or nonfiction, ask students to brainstorm with you what they'd like to learn about the topic. For example:

Writing about: the football game I went to last weekend

Questions we might wonder: Who was playing? Who won? What was the score? What was the most exciting part of the game?

Writing about: Dr. Seuss

Questions we might wonder: Is he real? Is that his real name? Is he alive? How did he start writing? How did he think up the weird stuff he wrote about?

Tell students that asking questions of themselves before they begin to write may help to more fully develop their writing pieces. Share that, "This should help to make your writing more satisfying to you and to others who might read what you've written!"

Other Ideas for Developing Ideas through Questioning

- Have follow-up lessons where you merely state topics you might consider for writing. Ask students, "If I write about this, what are some things you might want to know about this topic?" List the questions they come up with. Then, choose the one topic you feel is most interesting, based on the questions that seem most interesting. On some occasions, you might then use the questions to guide writing a piece, answering those questions that seem to fit.

- Make sure that students understand how details help to develop a piece of writing by adding to the clarity and interest in writing. Draw five geometric shapes on the board. Without telling which object you're describing, write a descriptive piece. Ask the students if it's developed well enough to identify the shape. You might give each partner group of students two similar objects (two rocks, two petals, two blades of grass, two torn strips of paper, etc.). Have them try to write about one of the objects in such detail that their partners can distinguish it from the other similar object. Teach them to do this by describing only one object, not two. For example, instead of saying, "It's the larger of the two petals," they might say, "It has a tiny bruise on the edge." This way students will notice details that will help to develop their ideas.

- Be sure to include informational topics in your mini-lessons of developing ideas and teaching students to develop ideas through questioning strategies. Science is a content area that is best taught through questioning and inquiry. Observe an experiment or some natural phenomenon and pause to ask questions about it. For example, the newspaper says there's going to be a meteor shower. Ask questions, such as: What are meteors? How are they formed? How fast do they travel? What should we expect to see? When will this occur? Search for answers and model how to write a piece based on the answers you discovered.

Mini-Lesson Focus: Writing Informational Text (Science)

Just as many students prefer to read nonfiction informational text, many students also favor writing about things that are factual and real. Science provides wonderful opportunities for a wide range of writing topics, creativity, and exploration. Content area writing, especially science, also allows for another dimension of writing where visuals and graphics might be used to illustrate and clarify the text. The illustrations and graphics might also help students to organize and summarize their text.

Choose a picture related to something you've been studying in science. The picture should be something with parts that can be labeled, such as a sprouting seed, a fish, a blood cell, phases of the moon, etc. To start your model lesson, either sketch the picture or copy a picture from a book onto a transparency, leaving space for writing.

As a review of what has been studied, have the students work with you to label the parts of the picture. Then, ask the students to help you summarize in a few words what the picture shows. For example:

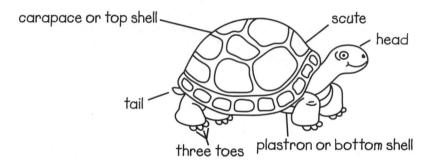

Now, next to the previous drawing sketch or copy a picture of a turtle with its shell closed. Have students help you label the parts of the picture. Tell students, "Now that we have our sketch, let's try to put into only a few words the main idea of what we've drawn. We have a picture of the turtle with its shell open, and a picture of how the turtle looks when it's folded up to protect itself. That's the main purpose of this illustration—to show how a turtle protects itself. So, let's put that as our title: The Three-Toed Box Turtle Protects Itself."

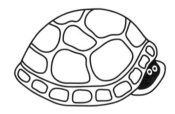

The Three-Toed Box Turtle Protects Itself

The step of determining the title of the picture helps students summarize the main point of what was studied.

If time allows or as a Day-Two lesson, explain the picture in sentences. Define the parts and elaborate on relationships between the parts. The picture will give structure to what is written.

The Three-Toed Box Turtle Protects Itself

The three-toed box turtle has a neat way of protecting itself. It has a top shell called a carapace and a bottom shell called a plastron. The bottom shell has a hinge, like you would find on a door. If the turtle is threatened, the bottom shell folds to seal together with the top shell. Then, the turtle is perfectly safe!

Information on three-toed box turtle from *Animal Defenses: How Animals Protect Themselves* by Etta Kaner (Kids Can Press, 1999).

Other Ideas for Writing Informational Text (Science)

- Model for students how to summarize major concepts into captions. Find pictures, charts, or illustrations in texts that you've read and/or studied in class. Reproduce these pictures on transparencies that you can share on your overhead projector. Think aloud about how these pictures represent big ideas in the text. Write a sentence that expresses the main concept or idea depicted across the bottom of the transparency. Try several of these, first modeling one yourself and then allowing students to try a couple along with you. This caption writing is a great way to teach students more about summarizing, drawing inferences, and writing with greater precision.

- Show students how to take notes from their science text as they read it, using a graphic organizer. Webs work well for this purpose. Place the major topic or chapter heading in the center of the map. Write subheadings in the next satellite bubbles. Add details in the next satellites.

- Carry the above note-taking lesson one step further. Without referring to the book, use the topic map outline to write a summary of what has been read. Turn the subheadings into main idea sentences and add the details (those in the third level satellites) to support the main ideas. This is information-processing inside out and a great study technique!

Mini-Lesson Focus: Writing Informational Text (Social Studies)

Third-graders are beginning to write more and more nonfiction. Previously, much of their writing revolved around writing first-person narratives and descriptions. They are now taught science and social studies content through curriculum textbooks. One way to "show what they know" is through informational writing. When you write to explain or share facts about a topic, you are writing in this mode. This type of writing usually includes a topic sentence, subtopics, supporting details and facts, and a conclusion. An orderly and sensible approach is used to inform the audience. Visuals, such as charts, tables, graphs, illustrations, photographs, and timelines are often used to support the social studies content.

Day One

"Today, I would like to think about writing a paragraph based on our social studies content. I think if I draw out the events in a sequence, then it will be easier for me to write the paragraph."

Select a topic (historical figure or event) studied in social studies. Sketch out a pictorial sequence of the facts.
For example:

Ask students to select an event or person studied in social studies and to draw a pictorial sequence of facts in order.

Day Two

"Now, I will continue using the social studies content and write a paragraph using the pictures as a guide for my writing. I will need to progress from left to right when I convert the illustrations into words. I will need a topic sentence, subtopics, supporting details, and a conclusion for my paragraph."

> The Pilgrims sailed from Europe to find a new life. They followed Christopher Columbus who sailed from Spain looking for a shorter trade route. The Pilgrims made the trip on a leaking ship, the <u>Mayflower.</u> The voyage was long and many of the Pilgrims became ill. They were brave to venture out on this dangerous journey. The Pilgrims were happy to be in a new place.

Check for a topic sentence, subtopics, supporting details, and a conclusion. Have students write a paragraph, using their pictorial sequence as a guide.

Other Ideas for Writing Informational Text (Social Studies)

• Model how to use a map where travels leading to the discovery of new lands in America are marked. Then, convert the map tracks into an orderly informational article.

• Model writing informational facts to include in a brochure about the history of the area where you live. Include facts on who founded the area, when it was founded, where the first people settled, why it was settled there, etc. After the information is gathered, students can design a brochure to incorporate all of the facts. The brochures can be displayed at the chamber of commerce, hotels, welcome centers, tourism office, etc. Students need an audience for their writing. It will be so exciting to see their brochures displayed.

• Often special vocabulary is included in social studies informational text. Model making a social studies dictionary to include these special words. As each unit is discussed, additional words can be added. The definition will come from the text and a sentence can be constructed that shows an understanding of the vocabulary word. The dictionary can be made from a 70-page notebook (spiral or sewn-in) that has been cut in half horizontally by a power saw (home builder's store) or a cutting blade (print shop). One example is a *Citizenship Unit Dictionary*:

- **citizen**: a person who belongs to a community or country and has rights and responsibilities

  A **citizen** should obey all of the laws.

- **freedom**: the right of people to make their own choices

  Many people come to our country searching for **freedom**

- **government**: a group of people who make the laws for a community or country

  The United States **government** has three branches.

- **vote**: a choice that gets counted

  A citizen should register to **vote**.

Mini-Lesson Focus: Writing Thank-You Notes

Students should be exposed to authentic purposes for writing. Many third-graders may be asked by their parents to write thank-you notes to their relatives for giving them presents. Third graders enjoy having an audience for their writing. Classroom experiences present many opportunities to write thank-you notes for real purposes.

Tell the students, "Well, boys and girls, we were so lucky to have Mrs. Jones come to our class yesterday. Do you think she would like to know how much we enjoyed the party? How could we let her know how we feel? We could call her on the phone, or we could write her a thank-you note. I think she would really appreciate a written note from each of you."

Bring in examples of thank-you notes that have been received. Discuss why these notes were written (for a wedding gift, for flowers sent, for a birthday present, etc.).

Determine the format most often used in these notes and sketch the format for the students.

```
                    Date

Greeting,

BodyBodyBodyBodyBody
BodyBodyBodyBodyBody
BodyBodyBodyBodyBody
BodyBodyBodyBodyBody
BodyBodyBodyBodyBody

            Closing,

            Signature
```

Model writing the thank-you note:

```
                                    September 20, 2002

Dear Mrs. Jones,

Thank you so much for the nice party. The food was delicious, and
the games were fun! We hope we were not too noisy. Please come
back to our classroom to see us soon.

                            Sincerely,

                            Mrs. White
```

Provide each student with a piece of stationery to write his or her own thank-you note, again for some authentic purpose. Allow them to observe you preparing the notes for mailing.

Provide a bank of words for students, such as this one for the note on page 72:

Mrs. Jones	favors	punch
food	games	party

Other Ideas for Writing a Thank-You Note

- Blank note templates can be provided to assist the students in writing the correct format. Having a supply on hand will encourage note writing.

- Students can brainstorm lists of people that they could refer to as an authentic audience for their notes. For example: teachers, friends, family, principal, food service staff, librarian, custodial staff, secretary, etc.

- Partner students to role-play performing good deeds for each other. The students will then write thank-you notes to their partners, thanking them for what they did.

- Ask students to write thank-you notes to other students in the school who may have done some kind deed for them.

Mini-Lesson Focus: Writing Friendly Letters

Students in third grade generally enjoy their social interactions with classmates, friends, and relatives. Writing letters to friends is a natural outgrowth of their desires to establish and maintain relationships. With a little guidance, students can produce some masterpieces and have fun, too!

Tell the students, "I want you to learn the art of writing letters to friends and learn that there are some tricks to writing good letters. First, we're going to learn some basics about writing friendly letters."

Certain formatting is expected and should be taught. (Remember not to overemphasize formatting to the extent that you ignore what's most important about letter writing. Formatting isn't really what a **good** letter is all about!) Tell students, "There are certain parts that all friendly letters have, and they each serve a good purpose. These parts have particular places where they must go on the stationery. Let me show you where the parts go and tell you why they are included in letters." Draw a diagram and point out each location as you explain, "The date goes here in the upper right hand corner. It's important to let your reader know when you wrote the letter so that they'll know when the news in your letter happened. The greeting of your letter makes it personal. It's like walking up to someone and saying, 'Hello!' The body of your letter is where all of your news goes. It's the reason you're writing the letter. The closing of your letter is like telling a friend 'Good-bye' on the phone or when you're parting. And, of course, it's important to identify who you are and give your letter a personal touch by signing your name. If you're really close to the person, you'll probably just sign it with your first name." Your diagram might look like this:

```
                              Date

        Greeting,

        BodyBodyBodyBodyBody
        BodyBodyBodyBodyBody
        BodyBodyBodyBodyBody
        BodyBodyBodyBodyBody
        BodyBodyBodyBodyBody

                        Closing,

                        Signature
```

Now that the format has been taught, the creative part begins! Friendly letters should be fun and full of personality. Show students two sample letters—one an obviously standard and rather boring letter, and another that uses a few tricks to make it interesting. Let the students read both and decide which one they'd rather receive from a friend. Which one is more fun to read? Which one has some personality?

Get students' ideas about why one letter might be more fun to receive than the other. If they don't mention these points, ask questions that would call attention to each point:

> "Do you think one writer shared more specific information than the other?"

> "Do you think one letter was more creative than another? What fun stuff was included?"

> "Did one writer seem to show more personal interest in the reader than the other?"

Encourage students to experiment with writing a letter to someone they know and to include these things which you'll list for them:

- Something fun for the reader (illustrations, clipped cartoons, a joke, etc.)

- Something that shows interest in the reader (ask questions that you want answered)

- Something specific that can be pictured in the reader's mind

- An interest that you and the reader have in common

Other Ideas for Writing Friendly Letters

- There are several books you can use to teach and encourage letter writing: the *Jolly Postman* series by Janet and Allan Ahlberg (books of letters) and *Yours Truly, Goldilocks* by Alma Flor Ada. Read one of these books for your mini-lesson and discuss what makes the letters good or bad.

- After you've taught your students about voice in their writing, point out that letters are ideal for letting their particular voices or writing personalities be heard.

- Be sure to teach students how to address their letters to others. Envelopes can be purchased very inexpensively for this purpose, or can be handmade by the students. Students should include the return address and the mailing address, using proper formatting. You may wish to keep a list of state abbreviations in the classroom.

- Brainstorm with students the types of questions they might ask in their letters to make their writing more interesting and more interactive. Have them work with partners to ask each other questions about things in their everyday lives: sports, interests, hobbies, favorite movies, favorite TV shows, family members, etc.

- Consider finding a class in another state that would become pen pals with your students. This is a way for students to learn about another community and another state firsthand. Provide time for letters to be written. Use the model lesson to remind students what a good letter includes. You might choose to write the pen pals' teacher for your model lessons.

Mini-Lesson Focus: Writing to Respond

There are many types of response writing. Often writing in response to a stated topic or prompt is done in the classroom to prepare students for a performance-based writing test. Many teachers feel guilty preparing students for these tests; however, they need not feel guilty about giving students an occasional prompt. This kind of writing is a "real life" task. In fact, think about how much of the writing you do that is in response to a specific request or a stated "assignment" or topic. For example, you write a grant to buy books for your classroom, your principal asks you to write an article for the school newsletter, or you must write a summary on a student's performance. Writing on demand is a "real life" task, and it's only fair that you should teach students to deal skillfully with such assignments.

Model writing on a topic similar to one that you want your students to be able to address. Tell students that there are some basics that they'll need to remember as they do this type of writing. These are the basics you should model for them:

Basic Rules for Test-Prompt Writing

Read the prompt carefully and think about what it says.

"Here's the prompt I'm going to address—'How to Take Care of a Pet.' Now, I need to think a few minutes about what the topic means. First, I notice that this is a 'how-to' topic. That means that I'll be explaining something. This won't be a story. I'll be giving information about taking care of a pet. I guess that I'll need to decide what kind of pet I know how to take care of. I'll want to write about something that I understand well. I think I'll write about caring for a dog since that's the pet I have."

Gather all the information you can that will help you.

"We'll want to read the test information carefully. Sometimes they tell us what they're looking for and how they'll grade our writing. Sometimes it says that you must show your planning or that you should check your writing carefully for errors. You'll want to pay close attention to all the information that's given to you."

Plan before you write.

"If the writing test tells us how we should plan, we'll use that as our guide. Sometimes it might be a topic map. If the test doesn't tell us how we must plan, we should remember all the different ways that we've learned to plan. We'll choose the one that we think will work best for us. I could make a jot list or an outline or a topic map. I think I'll use a topic map to get ready to write."

Think aloud as you plan your lesson, first adding main ideas and then details.

Writing Mini-Lessons for Third Grade: The Four-Blocks® Model © Carson-Dellosa CD-2419

Stick to the topic—no straying!

"After we read the topic and do our planning, we need to go back and check to be sure that we've stuck to the topic. All of our sentences need to relate to the topic."

Don't experiment! (This limitation is only necessary for test-taking conditions!)

"When we have our writing test, it's the time that we stick with our 'safe' writing. We don't experiment with fancy handwriting or with writing in shapes, which we sometimes do in our Writers' Workshop. We stick with things that we're pretty sure are correct."

Show what you know!

"When we have our writing test in the spring, it's the time that we get to 'show what we know.' That means we get to show all that we've learned throughout the year. We'll remember the basics about capital letters, end punctuation, commas, and sticking to the topic. We'll remember developing our ideas and keeping the reader interested in what we have to say. It's a time for us to let folks know how much we've grown as writers this year! We'll be proud of all that we're able to show!"

Other Ideas for Writing to Respond

- Writing to respond is often done to clarify students' thinking about content material in science, social studies, health, and math. Writing about what they've studied helps students to think about the material in a different way and to process the material. This type of response writing is usually fairly brief in length. In your mini-lesson, model how to address whatever prompt you're giving them to respond to. Model appropriate words to use for certain responses that require sequencing (first, next, then, last, after, later, etc.), content vocabulary, and transitional words. Model for them how to address the topic briefly. This type of response writing should require little or no pre-planning with jot lists or graphic organizers. Here are sample topics that students might be asked to write about related to different topics:

Math

- Explain how to add double-digit numbers in a series.

- Explain how to make an equilateral triangle.

- Explain what these division words mean: quotient, dividend.

- Write an example of how adding and subtracting dollars and cents might help you in everyday life.

Science

- Tell how you located the Big Dipper last night for your homework and draw a sketch of how it looked.

- Explain what **photosynthesis** means.

- Write briefly about what happens to the water in your bathtub as you get in and out (studying displacement).

Mini-Lesson Focus: Writing News Articles (Who, What, When, Where, Why)

Students need to learn a simple journalistic style of writing in third grade. Creating a classroom or school newsletter is the perfect format for a "real-life," authentic reason for writing and provides a real audience as well. News articles help students learn to organize and prioritize their factual writing. This format also provides an excellent opportunity for students to distinguish fact from opinion.

Day One

Search your local newspaper for a simple news article that can be read aloud to students and analyzed. Try to find an article that they can relate to or that is appealing in some way (funny or bizarre articles are usually a hit!). Also, be sure that the article clearly states the five W's (**who**, **what**, **when**, **where**, and **why**).

Take the article to your copy machine and enlarge the print if your copy machine has that function. Transfer the enlarged copy to a transparency.

Announce to the class, "Soon, we'll contribute news articles to a newsletter (or newspaper) that the class will produce. You'll all become reporters! But first, you'll need to learn how news writing is different from some of the other writing that we've done in class."

Show the news article on your overhead projector and read the article aloud to (or with) students.

Tell students, "News writing is sometimes called 'Five W' writing because reporters learn to tell the most important facts first in their articles. The five W's tell the **who**, **what**, **when**, **where**, and **why** of the story."

Ask students to help you find the five W's in the article you've just read. Use different colors of transparency pens to underline each of the five W's.

Day Two

As a model for students to follow, attempt writing your own news article about some school event that is familiar to the students. Define the event first.

Our Thanksgiving Food Drive

Next, determine the five W's of the event, thinking aloud as you recall these important elements. List each of the five W's on the transparency and jot down the information without attention to complete sentences.

Who?	Third-graders
What?	Collected canned goods at Thanksgiving
When?	First week of November
Where?	In our community
Why?	Some people don't have enough food

Stress to your students, "News articles move from the most to the least important information through the article. The five W's are the most important information. The least important information might be interviews, quotations, and reactions from people about the event."

Make a list of other things that readers might want to know about the food drive.

Other information I might include:

- What the principal said about the drive
- How many cans we collected
- Whose class collected the most cans
- Where the cans were taken

Day Three

Now, tell the students, "I'm ready to start putting my outline into complete sentences, starting with the five W's."

Write the news article:

Our Thanksgiving Food Drive

During the first week of November, third-grade students at Rosewood Elementary School collected food in the community for the people who are in need.

Continue with other details that you included in your brainstorming list. For example:

During the first week of November, third-grade students at Rosewood Elementary School collected food in the community for the people who are in need. Mrs. Smith's class brought the most cans—248. Students worked to pack all of the canned goods into boxes, and our principal took them to the food bank. Mr. Redford, the principal, said, "I am extremely proud of all of the third-graders!"

Begin to brainstorm with the students all of the different topics that might be included in the newspaper that your class will write. Soon assignments will be made to each class reporter, and they'll begin to follow the steps towards writing a good news article!

Other Ideas for Writing News Articles (Who, What, When, Where, Why)

- Try a lesson in which you compare the basic elements of news writing with those of narrative writing. With stories, the **who** is the main character(s); the **what** and **why** might be the problem/ conflict of the story; the **when** and **where** refer to the time and place of the setting. In narrative writing, however, the five W's aren't told as quickly. They are revealed slowly as the story unfolds. News writing is concise and the important elements are told quickly.

- Use news writing as an opportunity to teach students to conduct simple interviews to add information to their own articles. Choose a class or school event to use as the basis for your model lesson. Construct the beginning sentence with your five W's. Then, as a class, brainstorm a list of questions that could be asked about the event. Let the students ask a question or two to a partner. Teach them to record the quotes accurately. Then, have a few students share the answers they gathered. Show them how to incorporate the quotes or additional information into the article.

Mini-Lesson Focus: Writing Poetry (Using a Thesaurus, Rhyming Dictionary, and Other Resources)

Poetry is one text structure that third-graders are exposed to through read-alouds and through their own reading. They learn that poetry is usually concise, has images and sounds, may be free verse or rhyming, and has a main idea. Knowing this text structure in reading prepares them for writing poetry. A thesaurus, dictionary, and rhyming dictionary may be used as writing aids.

Tell the students, "I just love to read poetry. The images and sounds create an interesting picture in my mind. I love to read poetry out loud so I can hear the rhythm and sometimes rhyme. I am sure I can write poetry, too. Today, I am going to write an acrostic poem. I think I will use the season 'spring' as the topic. I need to think of an action verb phrase that begins with each letter of 'spring' that also relates to the topic. There are lots of interesting words I can use, but if I can't think of any I can always use a thesaurus or dictionary to help me. Let's see. The first letter of spring is 's', so some words I could use might be: snoring, swimming, swishing, or swinging." (Continue modeling other words for each letter.)

Model writing an acrostic poem. Demonstrate how to choose phrases that begin with each of the letters in a category that you and the students know a lot about (for example, the seasons, holidays, personal names, etc.). Brainstorm what comes to mind when we think of the spring season. The first word in each of the phrases of this poem is a verb showing action. Generating many action verbs that begin with each of the letters before writing makes the actual writing much easier. Writing poetry should be fun and entertaining to read aloud, but remember how important it is that talk **precedes** writing. Model using a thesaurus to aid in word choices.

SPRING

Swinging from the tree

Playing in the park

Running through the grass

Imagining summer vacation

Nodding off to sleep

Grabbing fireflies

Ask students to write their own acrostic poems using phrases. Be sure to allow an opportunity for the poems to be read aloud either to the whole class or to a partner. The rhythm or rhyme heard orally sometimes motivates a reluctant writer to see herself as a writer.

Other Ideas for Writing Poetry

- Another type of acrostic poem can be written using adjectives instead of phrases. When students are asked to write about something they know a lot about, you can be sure that using their names as topics will work! Using a thesaurus and/or dictionary will help in generating many interesting adjectives that begin with each of the letters of their names.

MELISSA

Musical

Energetic

Lovely

Interesting

Sensitive

Sensible

Active

- Write poems using digraphs and blends studied in the Working with Words Block. Model writing these letter poems using a thesaurus and a rhyming dictionary. Discuss how they will need three words that begin with the same letter pattern and a different word that rhymes with the second word chosen.

Sh	Ch
Is for shaggy	Is for children
Sh is for shady	Ch is for chief
Sh is for shawls	Ch is for chicken
For the nice lady	To eat with beef

This is a variation of writing silly sentences. Students will find writing these types of poems quite amusing!

- Third-graders also enjoy writing tongue twisters with rhythmic patterns. Increase the number of words in each line. A dictionary and a rhyming dictionary serve as good resources.

Bluebird

Bubbly Bluebird

Brainy Bubbly Bluebird

Braggy Brainy Bubbly Bluebird

Batty Braggy Brainy Bubbly Bluebird

Mini-Lesson Focus: Teaching that Verb Tense Is Important

Third-graders have learned so much about the syntax of our language. Much of their knowledge is a result of natural acquisition—hearing and seeing good models of grammar and usage. For some students the use of correct grammar comes naturally. They've had consistent modeling from parents and others around them. They may not necessarily be able to explain why certain words are considered "correct" and others "incorrect," but, for the most part, they use them correctly. For other students who have not had adequate exposure to strong models of proper language usage, your daily modeling will be critical in helping them to develop a sense of correct syntax.

Write a short composition where the time (past, present, or future) on which tenses are based is obvious. Keep the piece short for this part of the lesson. For example, tell students, "Today, I think I'll write a story about a dog I had when I was nine years old."

Write about the dog:

Punjab

When I was nine years old, I had a huge, fluffy, black English Shepherd that we called Punjab. Punjab thought that his job was to keep me safe from harm, and he took his job very seriously. If someone new walked in our yard, Punjab quickly backed them out of the yard unless I patted him on the head and said, "It's okay, Punjab!" He was always on alert to keep me safe!

Tell the students, "I want to show you something about verbs that you should think about in your writing. Many verbs change with the time. In the piece I just wrote, I am an adult talking about an experience from long ago. Now let me try an experiment and rewrite this paragraph as if I'm no longer an adult. I'm going to pretend that Punjab is a dog I have now and see how this piece changes."

Now read back over your piece and think aloud as you strike through and change certain words.

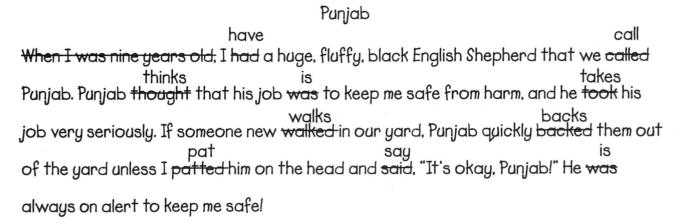

Conclude by telling students, "Be mindful of the verbs you use and what those verbs say about the time you're referring to in your writing."

Other Ideas for Teaching that Verb Tense Is Important

- After modeling the introductory lesson for verb tense, include in your think-aloud your rationale for using a certain verb tense. For example, you might say, "Now if I say that **I walk** today, I'll need to say **walked** if it was yesterday or in the past. So often we add an **–ed** for verbs that talk about something that happened in the past."

- Have fun experimenting with content material, especially from history-related topics that will stress past, present, and future. Write about what happened "back then" and then transform it to the present. After writing both similar pieces, go back and emphasize why verbs changed.

The First Thanksgiving (Then)

America's first Thanksgiving <u>was</u> in 1621. This <u>was</u> a celebration of a good harvest. The Pilgrims <u>were</u> happy that they <u>had farmed</u> on their new land and <u>had grown</u> bountiful crops. The Native Americans <u>were</u> already there when the Pilgrims <u>came</u> from England, and they <u>helped</u> the Pilgrims <u>farm</u> their crops. The Pilgrims <u>invited</u> the Native Americans to their feast. They <u>shared</u> together in the first American Thanksgiving feast and <u>gave</u> thanks.

The First Thanksgiving (Now)

Our first Thanksgiving celebration <u>is</u> today! We <u>have been</u> busy <u>farming</u> our land and <u>growing</u> our crops. The Native Americans <u>are teaching</u> us new things that we <u>need</u> to know about farming in this country. Today we <u>will cook</u> our vegetables and fruit and <u>will serve</u> our food with our new friends. We <u>will</u> all <u>give</u> thanks at our feast for our good fortune.

Note: Be as "forgiving" as possible about the use of correct verb tenses in writing at the third-grade level. The nuances of correctness are really far beyond the comprehension of many, if not most third-graders. The rules are complex and sophisticated, and there are so many irregularities. Offer students your very best models of written and spoken language and include your rationales in your think-alouds. They'll soon begin to acquire a sense of correctness through this exposure.

Mini-Lesson Focus: Using Pronouns (Replacing Pronouns with Precise Words— Beginning of Sentences)

Because third-graders often write personal narratives, they fall into the trap of overusing personal pronouns, especially the pronoun I, as sentence openings. Unless they are asked to focus on the beginning word of each sentence, many are quilty of this abuse.

Tell the students, "I enjoy writing stories about myself and things that happen to me. When I write this type of story, I have to be careful not to use the word 'I' too often. My writing will be more interesting if I find other words to use in place of this pronoun."

Model writing a personal story about any topic (family, friends, vacations, trips, etc.). The overuse of the pronoun I should be evident in the story. Circle the first word in each sentence and then list the words in the margin of the overhead so that the overuse is clear to the children.

Swimming in the Summer

Ⓘlike to go swimming in the summer.Ⓘtⓘis hot, and the water cools me off.Ⓘlike to swim under the water.Ⓘlike to jump off the diving board.Ⓘdon't like to dive because water gets up my nose.Ⓘswim and swim untilⓘget tired.Ⓣhen I sit on the side of the pool until I am ready to swim again.

Model other options for beginning words. Show students how revision can make their writing better. All of the pronouns will not need to be replaced.

Swimming in the Summer

Swimming in the summer is great. When it is so hot, the water cools me off. Swimming under the water is fun. I like to jump off the diving board. Water gets up my nose when I dive. I swim and swim until I get tired. Then, I sit on the side of the pool until I am ready to swim again.

Have the students analyze the beginnings of the sentences in a piece already written.

Other Ideas for Using Pronouns (Pronoun/Antecedent Agreement)

- A pronoun (a word used in place of one or more nouns) must agree with its antecedent, the noun to which the pronoun refers.

  Use an example of a previous year's third-grade writing or a sample that you've written. Give each student a copy. Model on the overhead how to draw a red line from the noun to the pronoun that replaces the noun. Circle the noun and pronoun if they don't agree. Tell the students to continue this activity in the piece of writing.

  Susan is my friend. She is funny.

- Allow students to go to a writing center and put on the "Editor's Visor." (This can be made from an inexpensive plastic visor with the word "Editor" written on it with paint pens.) Have a visor in the center for each of the children allowed to be there at one time. These editors will now hunt for pronouns and noun agreement. The students will have fun seeing who can find them all.

- Ask students to find pictures in magazines that show nouns (people, places, objects). With a partner, students can write on a sticky note the pronoun that would replace the noun. The partners would then write sentences about the picture using the correct pronouns.

- Write common pronouns on index cards (**I**, **me**, **you**, **he**, **him**, **she**, **her**, **it**, **we**, **us**, **you**, **they**, and **them**). Students will enjoy drawing a card and illustrating the noun or object the pronoun could represent.

Mini-Lesson Focus: Using Commas in a Series

It is important to explain to the students why it is necessary to use commas correctly. Commas help readers know when to pause. The students must understand how to use commas between words or groups of words in a series, including before the words **and** or **or**. For example: The boys played football, soccer, kickball, and volleyball while at camp.

Tell the students, "Sometimes I need to use commas in my writing, but I am not always sure where they should go. I remember when I was making a list of possible presents for my daughter's birthday, and I had to think how each item needed to be separated by a comma. A comma was also needed before the words **and** or **or**. Then, I remembered how to write this sentence. 'Tomorrow is Susan's birthday. I need to shop for a present, but she has asked for too many things. She wants a new purse, a sweater, a necklace, and a hair dryer. I will have to decide what she really needs!' Now this sentence can be read easily since the commas separate each item."

Share a third-grader's paragraph where a series of words or groups of words are used. The children love to read each other's writing. Of course, this writing should not be from a student presently in the class.

Lunchtime

One of my favorite times of the school day is lunchtime. I can't wait to see if pizza spaghetti hot dogs fish or chicken nuggets will be served. Because I like them all, I won't be disappointed. While eating, we can talk with our friends sit quietly or read a book. This special time of day goes by too quickly.

Read the paragraph aloud without pausing between words in a series.

Ask the students to edit the student writing with you by putting in commas where needed. Use different colored markers for commas between words and commas between groups of words.

Lunchtime

One of my favorite times of the school day is lunchtime. I can't wait to see if pizza, spaghetti, hot dogs, fish, or chicken nuggets will be served. Because I like them all, I won't be disappointed. While eating, we can talk with our friends, sit quietly, or read a book. This special time of day goes by too quickly.

Suggest that the students write a paragraph that requires a series of words to be used. Some students will try to write a series, but some will just write something they want to tell you about. Over time, students should be able to demonstrate the correct use of this skill. Possible topics include:

Things We Do in School

Sunday Is My Favorite Day Because...

Things I Would Like to Know About Fourth Grade

Presents I Would Like to Give Mom or Dad

Writing Mini-Lessons for Third Grade: The Four-Blocks® Model

Add to the Editor's Checklist:

8.   I have used commas correctly.

Other Ideas for Using Commas in a Series

• Partner students and have them read their paragraphs aloud to each other. Tell them not to pause after each word in a series. Reread the paragraph aloud, this time pausing after each word in a series. Help the students see how the use of commas in a series helps the writer communicate more clearly with the reader. Auditory learners need to hear this difference as well as see it.

• Kinesthetic learners may have more success if they cut apart sentences that contain words in a series. Sentences can be written on sentence strips for this purpose. For example, write and cut apart the following sentence:

Sally likes to read books about cats, hamsters, and parakeets.

Model writing on the sentence strip, cutting the words in a series apart, and then reconstructing the sentence. Give sentence strips to the students and allow them to write their own sentences for this activity.

Mini-Lesson Focus: Using Apostrophes in Contractions

Using apostrophes correctly in writing is part of language arts standards in many states. One common use of apostrophes is when writing contractions. A contraction is a shortened form of writing two words as one word. The apostrophe (') is used where letters have been omitted.

Tell the students, "I think I would like to tell you about how much I like to cook for a party. I have had graduation parties for my two girls and anniversary parties for my parents. Sometimes I invite family and friends over for birthdays, too. Often, we will have company over for no special reason and I enjoy throwing together party food. As I tell you about this, I will probably use lots of contractions in my writing. I will try to use the apostrophe in the correct place."

Model the correct use of this skill by writing a paragraph telling the students about something that interests you. Use as many different types of contractions as possible.

Cooking for a Special Party

Cooking is fun and exciting if you have a party for a special occasion. Graduations and anniversaries are occasions when I like to cook. A special cake isn't the only treat I'll serve. Wouldn't you like chips, roasted nuts, brownies, and sugar cookies, too? I've also served banana punch to drink. Many guests leave with this recipe because they're sure they'll make it for their parties. As you can see, I'm happy when it's time to cook for a special party.

Isolate the contractions by circling them and making a list to add to a contractions chart. (Contractions to circle in the paragraph above: **isn't**, **I'll**, **wouldn't**, **I've**, **they're**, **they'll**, **I'm**, and **it's**.) Discuss what two words the contractions stand for. Note the letters that the apostrophe replaces. Tell the students to use some contractions as they write today. Add new contractions to the chart.

Other Ideas for Using Apostrophes in Contractions

- Create a contractions chart developed from the model lesson. Insert each contraction listed from the paragraph in a form such as the one below. Model writing a sentence using the contractions correctly. Ask the students to continue to fill in the form.

Contraction	Long Form	Sentence
isn't	is not	Our classroom isn't large enough.
I'll	I will	Tomorrow I'll go to school.

- After completing the contractions chart, instruct the students to cut apart each box. With a partner these can be mixed up and then reconstructed. Provide an envelope as a container for the words. Allow the students to take these contraction words and sentences home to share with their parents as a homework assignment.

- Model writing a persuasive paragraph using contractions. Ask the students to write on a persuasive topic and to use at least three contractions. Possible topics include:

    Persuade the cafeteria staff to serve your favorite meal.

    Persuade your parents to increase your allowance.

    Persuade your brother or sister to do your chores for one week.

Mini-Lesson Focus: Using Apostrophes with Possessive Nouns

A common use of the apostrophe is when writing possessive nouns. Possessives are formed to show ownership. Whether you use singular or plural nouns, determine where the apostrophe should be placed in the possessive word.

Singular:

Melissa's car

the dress's ribbon

Plural:

the boys' playhouse

the chairs' cushions

the oxen's yoke

Tell the students, "On Sunday, I went with my family to my aunt's house. She lives about an hour away from us. I think I'd like to tell you about some of the country scenes along the way. As I write I will probably use some possessive nouns, and I will have to be careful about where to put the apostrophe. I know that if the noun is singular I add the apostrophe, then the **s,** and if the noun is plural and ends in an **s** the apostrophe goes after the **s**. Let me begin to tell you about this Sunday afternoon drive, and I will think about how to use the apostrophe with possessive nouns."

Model using the apostrophe correctly in possessive nouns.

Going for a Drive

Driving in the country is a peaceful way to spend an hour or two. As you look around you can see the trees' leaves on the ground. The farmer's cows are lying in the pasture. The edge of the pond is covered with goose feathers. The only sound is the motor of Mr. Jones's tractor. The drive goes by quickly because of the country scenes.

Ask the students to assist you in identifying the types of possessive nouns used and how to use the apostrophe correctly. Use different colors of markers to circle the possessive noun types. Ask students to write about something they would like to tell you and to use possessives if possible. Possible topics include:

Description of a Mountain Scene
Flying Kites
Activities with Friends
Rainy Days

Ask the students to read their paragraphs aloud to partners. The partner listens for possessive nouns and writes them using the apostrophe correctly.

Add to the Editor's Checklist:

9.   I have used apostrophes correctly.

Writing Mini-Lessons for Third Grade: The Four-Blocks® Model

Other Ideas for Using Apostrophes with Possessive Nouns

• Reread excerpts from favorite books. Ask the children to listen for possessive nouns and to write them as they are heard. Divide the class into two groups. For example:

  • girls and boys
  • table 1/table 2 and table 3/table 4
  • left side of the room and right side of the room

  Then, award points to those students who write the correct number of possessive nouns.

• Prepare a transparency with an excerpt from a book, magazine, or other text and cover the possessive nouns. On the overhead, model writing in the possessive noun using the apostrophe correctly. Then, uncover the author's original words and compare with your own words.

• Write a paragraph that uses both possessive nouns and contractions. For the class, model how these two uses of the apostrophe are alike and different.

Mini-Lesson Focus: Using a Variety of Sentences (Combining)

For writing to be interesting it should include a variety of sentences. Sentences of different lengths and of various types will engage the reader. Students should avoid writing list-like, short, choppy sentences. When combining sentences, choose from the following connecting words: **and**, **although**, **because**, **but**, **or**, **so**.

Tell the students, "Today I would like to show you a piece of writing that is not very interesting. As we look at this writing, it is clear that the sentences are too short and choppy! Let's read this paragraph about a visit to grandmother's house and see if I can change or combine the sentences to make the writing more interesting."

Use a piece of student writing or model writing a piece of your own that is uninteresting because of its short, choppy sentences.

A Visit to Grandmother's House

On Sunday I visited my grandmother. We had fun. We went for a walk. We picked flowers. She cooked my favorite foods. I inhaled every bite. We played the old organ. I sang along. I plan to visit her again next month.

With the help of the class, change types of sentences and combine sentences to make the writing more interesting.

A Visit to Grandmother's House

Have you ever had a perfect day? I have. On Sunday I visited my grandmother. We had fun when we went for a walk and picked flowers. When she cooked my favorite foods for lunch, I inhaled every bite!! I sang along when we played the old organ. You can bet that I will return for a visit next month for another perfect day!

Have students write a paragraph with the purpose of varying the sentences.

Other Ideas for Using a Variety of Sentences

- Select literature as an example of how an author's writing is more interesting when sentences are varied. Some titles include:

  Because of Winn-Dixie by Kate DiCamillo (Candlewick Press, 2001).

  More Than Anything Else by Marie Bradby (Orchard Books, 1995).

  Today Was a Terrible Day by Patricia Reilly Giff (Puffin Books, 1980).

- Allow the students to select a piece of their previously completed writing. Instruct them to apply the information about sentence variety to this piece. Many times students are able to make their writing better by changing the types of sentences or by combining sentences to vary the lengths.

- When students begin sentences with the word **and**, it is often a clue that they are ready to combine sentences. Many times by only changing punctuation and capital letters, a more interesting sentence will emerge.

First time:

My friend, Jeff, is a football player. And he plays on the *Saluda River* team. When he plays, he throws the ball at least 20 yards. And he can also catch the ball on the run! He can do it all! Jeff kicks the ball high in the air. And he runs very fast. Jeff is an awesome athlete.

Possible rewrite:

My friend, Jeff, is a football player, and he plays on the *Saluda River* team. When he plays, he throws the ball at least 20 yards, and he can also catch the ball on the run! He can do it all! Jeff kicks the ball high in the air, and he runs very fast. Jeff is an awesome athlete.

Later in Third Grade–Getting Better

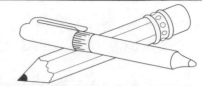

Mini-Lesson Focus: Writing Good First Lines

Many students say that the toughest part of writing is getting a piece started—just getting a good first sentence on the paper. You can do much to help students relieve their first sentence anxiety.

Tell the students, "Many famous writers say that they often rewrite the first lines of their stories many times before they're satisfied that they've found just the right words. Writers have many decisions to make about their first sentences. The main question they ask is, 'What do I want to accomplish with my first sentence?'

There are many different purposes that can be served with the very first sentence of a story. I'm going to write some of these purposes on the chalkboard (or a transparency)."

A first sentence in narrative text can:

- Begin to describe the setting.

- Begin to describe the main character(s).

- Begin to define the problem in the story.

- Catch the reader's attention. (This one is called a "hook.")

Tell the students, "I'm going to try an experiment that I want you to participate in. I'm going to read the first lines of several stories. I want you to think about the lines and what the author might be trying to accomplish. I want you to write down on a sheet of paper your opinion of the purpose after I read the line, then we'll talk about them."

Students will enjoy working together with partners or small groups to make their decisions. Read 3–5 first lines. Allow students a few minutes to discuss with their partner or group after you've read each first line. Have them write down the purpose in a word or two. Call on each partner group or small group and record their answers. Ask them to support their answers.

Here are some good examples, although you can use any story:

"This is the great/Kapiti Plain,/All fresh and green/from the African rains"

Bringing the Rain to Kapiti Plain by Verna Aardema (Dial Books for Young Readers, 1991).

Likely Purpose: establish setting

"Once upon a time there was a farmer who had but one horse."

"The One-Horse Farmer" by Sally Derby (*Spider* magazine, February 1999).

Likely Purpose: hinting at conflict/problem in the story

Writing Mini-Lessons for Third Grade: The Four-Blocks® Model

"Life was going along okay when my mother and father dropped the news."

Superfudge by Judy Blume (Econo-Clad Books, 1999).

Likely purpose: hook, anticipation

"On a night when the moon was full of itself, full of restless dreams and wide-awake thoughts, a girl by the name of Firen could not sleep."

Moonflute by Audrey Wood (Harcourt, 1986).

Likely purpose: introducing character, hinting at problem in story

Tell students to think about their own first lines as they write. "What impression do you want to make with the reader?"

Other Ideas for Writing Good First Lines

• After students have understood and practiced first lines in narrative text, do the same activity with expository/informational text. The main purposes served by expository text are to:

   • Catch the reader's attention. (Again, called a "hook.")

   • State what the subject of the text is.

Some good first lines and texts for this activity are:

"The bald eagle is a magnificent bird."

The Bald Eagle by Patricia Ryon Quiri (Children's Press, 1998).

"A snake has a long body and no legs."

Amazing Snakes by Alexandra Parsons (Knopf Publishing, 1990).

"Picture a huge dinosaur standing in front of you."

Tyrannosaurus Rex by Elaine Landau (Children's Press, 1999).

• After students have practiced the first line exercise with narrative and expository texts, try this activity during your mini-lesson time. Tell students to listen carefully as you read some first lines. You want them to try to guess from the first lines only whether the texts are narratives/stories or expository/informational texts. You might even turn this mini-lesson into a competition between cooperative groups of students. Read aloud a line for each group and give the group a point if they guess correctly. If a group makes an incorrect guess, the next group can reply and earn the point. Students will benefit greatly from hearing so many good first lines and from thinking about how authors get started.

Mini-Lesson Focus: Using Powerful Verbs

After students at third-grade level have become more fluent in their writing, they are usually ready to learn to make their writing more vivid, exciting, and powerful. Although we'll stress the use of adjectives that will bring more life to their words, we'll also want to emphasize how verbs can be used for that same purpose.

Write a piece that allows for the use of action verbs. Use action verbs in your first draft that are nondescript.

The Last Basket

After three hours of watching a game that was constantly close, I was sad that my team was down two points with just a few seconds on the scoreboard. All at once, number 23 took the ball right out of the hands of a surprised opposing team member's hands at mid-court. Our fans all looked at the clock and immediately began to count down the final six seconds, wondering if the game could possibly still be won. Number 23 dribbled the ball for a few steps, and then turned to position himself for the shot.

"Four...three..." we all said out loud as we reminded him of the time remaining.

Number 23's arms pushed the ball with all of his strength. We watched as the ball went through the air, higher and higher, until it went in the basket! We jumped from our seats as the scoreboard reported three additional points to our score. We had won a hard-fought game!

Announce that, "Although I like the piece I've written today, I still feel that I can make it a little better by replacing some of the verbs. Sometimes verbs are weak or boring when they should be strong and exciting. I definitely need as many strong, powerful, exciting verbs in this piece as I can find."

Here are the kinds of changes you might propose. There's no need to try to change all of the verbs—just a few!

After three hours of watching a game that was constantly close, I was sad that

my team was down two points with just a few seconds on the scoreboard. All at

snatched

once, number 23 ~~took~~ the ball right out of the hands of a surprised opposing team

stared

member's hands at mid-court. Our fans all ~~looked~~ at the clock and immediately began

to count down the final six seconds, wondering if the game could possibly still be won.

pounded

Number 23 ~~dribbled~~ the ball for a few steps, and then turned to position himself for

the shot.

                                     screamed
"Four...three..." we all ~~said~~ out loud as we reminded him of the time remaining.

                              launched
Number 23's arms ~~pushed~~ the ball with all of his strength. We watched as the ball

sailed   leaped
~~went~~ through the air, higher and higher, until it went in the basket! We ~~jumped~~ from our

seats as the scoreboard reported three additional points to our score. We had won

a hard-fought game!

Read back through your story and ask the students if they agree that the verb changes made the writing a little more exciting. Hopefully they'll agree! Remind them to think about powerful verbs when they write.

Other Ideas for Using Powerful Verbs

• Choose a book that you consider to have powerful verbs to read aloud during your Self-Selected Reading Block. Then, bring the story into your Writing Block. Read back through some of the pages and record with the students the verbs they hear that are powerful. Make a chart in the classroom to which you regularly add powerful verbs that you find during classroom reading. The students can then use this chart to make some verb choices when they write.

• Brainstorm with your students a list of all different verbs without any restrictions of action, being, or any particular context. Then, take a vote about each of the verbs as to whether or not they consider it to be a powerful (descriptive, exciting, etc.) verb. Cross out the verbs that aren't considered strong. You might take this a step further by allowing an additional vote as to the strongest of all the verbs or the top three most powerful verbs of those on your list. This helps students to become more discriminating in their choice of words in general, and verbs more specifically.

• Encourage students to move away from their overuse of verbs of being (**is**, **are**, **were**, etc.). Some use of these verbs is necessary, but overuse can be a weakness of writing. Give students some simple examples of how they can reword sentences to get rid of weak verbs.

He is a football player.   He plays football.

She is a writer of novels.   She writes novels.

• After several mini-lessons in which you have stressed active, powerful verbs, try giving students a chance to insert more descriptive verbs in the context of something that has been written. Write a sample of your own. Reproduce it for each student. Let students work as partners or in small groups to replace some of the verbs. Then, read back through your writing and ask for suggestions that students have come up with. Let students decide whether they think a change should be made and which word they think works best.

Note: Stress that your goal is to change only the words that will make the writing sound better. Sometimes too many "big" words can be distracting.

Mini-Lesson Focus: Discovering Voice in Writing

Helping students develop a voice in their writing can be a difficult task. Difficult, that is, until you show them that they already have a distinct writing voice—their very own—and that they have learned to use it without being taught.

Day One

Tell the students, "Writers' Workshop will be a little different today. Instead of continuing what you've been working on or starting a new piece independently, you're going to 'talk' to each other today."

Share several rules that they must observe:

- No words can be spoken aloud. Everything you want to say to someone should be written on paper.

- You may get up from your desk to deliver your notes and then quickly be re-seated.

- Try to include everyone at your table in your written discussions. (You may want to encourage them to have one "discussion" circulating in their cooperative groups and then any additional discussions they wish to have. This will ensure that everyone is engaged.)

- You can write about anything you want to, but you shouldn't write things on the notes that can't be read by the teacher or things that aren't kind.

- Keep as many conversations going as you can.

- Don't worry about spelling, grammar, and that sort of thing!

Tell the students exactly how much time they'll have for "conversing," and set a timer to signal when they should stop. 15–20 minutes may be a reasonable amount of time to allow—or certainly longer if your students are particularly "talkative."

As the time begins, you'll want to take part in the conversations. Quickly write a note and pass it to a student. Without waiting for a reply, write another one and pass it to someone else. Pay close attention to children who might be left out by others, and keep them busy writing to you. Get the ball rolling with comments like: "Hey, Zack! How did your ball game go yesterday? Hope your team won!!!", "Jill, how's your baby brother getting along? Do you enjoy helping with him?", "Bobby, what's your favorite book that you've read this year?" etc.

When the time is up, ask students to discuss the following question in their cooperative group. They should record their responses on a piece of paper. The responses will be used for the next day's mini-lesson. The question is: What are all the things you notice that are different in your note-writing from the other writing we usually do in class?

Ask students to turn in any notes they don't mind being read. You'll use a few in the Day Two lesson.

Writing Mini-Lessons for Third Grade: The Four-Blocks® Model

Day Two

Ask students for their responses to the question that was posed at the end of the Day One lesson. List their responses on the board or on an overhead transparency. Responses should include such things as: **We didn't pay attention to punctuation. Sometimes we wrote words all in capital letters. Sometimes we underlined words. Sometimes we put lots of exclamations points or question marks. We used lots of contractions. We wrote more like we talk.** (If students don't list these, ask if anyone noticed any of these things in the notes they wrote or received.)

Explain to students that the kind of writing they do in their notes shows their writing "voices." Voice makes writing more interesting. It's the way we show expression and add interest to our writing. It's how writing, just like people, has personality.

Using some of the notes collected from the previous day (or using the examples below), try writing simple translations to show voice vs. lifeless writing.

Voice from notes: What's up?

Lifeless writing: How are you?

Voice from notes: I can't <u>BELIEVE</u> you said that!

Lifeless writing: Why did you say that?

Voice from notes: Wow!!!! I LOVE going to the fair!

Lifeless writing: The fair is fun.

Give students time to write self-selected pieces after the mini-lessons. Remind them to use their voices in their own writing.

Other Ideas for Discovering Voice in Writing

- Have students construct cartoon storyboards where dialogue spoken by characters and illustrated in the story is more likely to express "down to earth" language. Carry these storyboards a step further and have students translate the drawings and dialogue into actual stories where the language remains expressive.

- Following up on the "translations" in the Day 2 lesson for voice, see if students can translate writing that has no voice into lively, expressive writing. Taking a "dry" content textbook (unfortunately, they do exist in abundance), have students work in partners, in small groups, or as a class during your mini-lesson time, to "liven-up" excerpts from the text. They may thoroughly enjoy retelling the writing of *The Declaration of Independence* or of the life of an amoeba with some pizzazz!

Mini-Lesson Focus: Avoiding Overuse of Certain Words

Once students have gained confidence in their abilities to communicate in writing and have become at least somewhat fluent, they will likely need to refine their writing. One of the first items of revision will be to improve word choices. Third-graders often fall into a habit of overusing certain words, likely the words they feel comfortable using. Some gentle nudging from you might be what greatly improves their vocabularies and encourages some exploration of word choices. In third grade, one word that seems to be overused consistently is the word **said**. This is probably because third-grade students are using so much more dialogue in their writing. Let's find a way to zap the dull words and add more excitement to their writing!

In your model lesson for the day, write a composition and purposefully overuse the word **said**.

Concert in the Park

My husband and I took our children to the park for a concert one Sunday afternoon. This was when the girls were ages 5 and 8. We spread our blanket on the ground, opened our picnic basket, and lazily began to eat and enjoy the concert.

"I see a big black cloud," Caroline, the 5-year-old said, but none of us paid attention.

"I see more black clouds," she said again.

"Honey, the clouds aren't going to bother you, and the weather forecast didn't call for rain today," I said back to her.

In a little while, she said again, "But, the clouds are darker now. I'm scared."

"Come and sit in my lap and listen to the music," my husband said to her.

"I want to go home," she finally said.

Before long, a few drops of rain fell. We still weren't alarmed, but began to pack our picnic basket just in case. As we did, we said, "We won't melt, though, so don't worry!"

About that time, a thundering crack of lightning hit a tree behind where the band was playing.

"You hold onto Beth, and I'll carry Caroline and the basket! Let's make a run for the car!" my husband said.

By the time we got to the car, both children were in tears, and we were all soaking wet. "Next time, Caroline," I said, "we'll listen to your weather forecast!"

After completing the composition, ask students what they think would make your writing better, adding something like, "When I read it back, there seems to be something distracting me." Make the overuse fairly obvious so that students will make the discovery, but, of course, if all else fails, suggest that you think that you've used a particular word too often. (Still no response? Abandon deductive exploration and tell them that you've used **said** way too often in this piece!)

Ask them to help you go back through your writing and substitute more expressive words for the many **said**s. Guide them by asking questions such as, "How do you think she/he/I said that?" "What do you think he/she/I was feeling as he/she/I said that?" Sometimes it's good to have a discussion about which might be the better of two words that have been suggested. As new words are decided upon, strike through each **said** and write the new word above it, just as you would expect the students to do on their papers. Use the chart below for some good substitutions.

You may want to have the class construct a chart to hang in the room with lists of words to use instead of **said**. This would be a great resource for them throughout the year! Caution them, of course, not to randomly choose a word from the chart, but to be sure that it is appropriate for the context of their writing. Here are some words to use instead of **said**:

replied	answered	responded	remarked
asked	inquired	demanded	stated
cried	begged	pleaded	growled
requested	explained	snapped	questioned
whimpered	bragged	screamed	yelled
whispered	snarled	screeched	laughed

Add to the Editor's Checklist:

      10.   I have made wise word choices.

Other Ideas for Avoiding Overuse of Certain Words

• After the lesson, assign each cooperative group in the class a word that is commonly overused. Challenge them to brainstorm a healthy list of words that can be substituted. Allow them to use a thesaurus and a dictionary to aid in their word search. After some input from you concerning the charts (to be sure that students understand nuances of certain words and their appropriate uses), display the charts in the room in your writing center or some place where they can be easily accessed during writing. Some of the words commonly overused are: **good, nice, said, pretty, mean, best,** and **bad.**

Mini-Lesson Focus: Using Transitional Words and Phrases

"How do I help my students move away from short, choppy sentences that do not appear to be connected?" This question is asked many times over by third-grade teachers. A writing device used to achieve a smooth flow from one sentence to the next is transition. This transition may connect words or phrases that show relationships.

Brainstorm transition words that would more often be used by third-graders. A possible list would be: **and, also, in addition, but, however, therefore, at the same time, finally,** and **then**.

Model writing a paragraph where transition words and phrases are needed but are not written in the paragraph.

Tell the students, "I think I will tell you about a trip to the Riverbanks Zoo that I recently went on. The exhibits were so interesting, and I would like to tell you about the gorillas and the flamingos. Because I visited several exhibits, I will probably need to use some transition words so that there is a smooth flow to my writing."

> My trip to the zoo was so interesting. I went to see the new gorilla exhibit. The gorillas were not in the observation room. I walked back to this exhibit. I saw them in the grassy area. I decided to see the flamingos. There wasn't much going on. I visited the sea lions to watch the 3:00 feeding. It was time to go home because it was closing time. My visit to the zoo was fun.

Read the paragraph aloud and ask the students to listen for short and choppy sentences. Discuss how the addition of transition words from the brainstorm list will improve the writing.

Insert transition words using a different color of marker.

> My trip to the zoo was so interesting. First, I went to see the new gorilla exhibit, but the gorillas were not in the observation room. Later, I walked back to this exhibit and I saw them in the grassy area. Then, I decided to see the flamingos. However, there wasn't much going on. In addition, I visited the sea lions to watch the 3:00 feeding. Finally, it was time to go home because it was closing time. My visit to the zoo was fun.

Reread the paragraph and assist the students in identifying sentences that now flow smoothly.

Have students select a first draft that was previously written. Let them use red pens or crayons to insert transition words that will eliminate short, choppy sentences.

Other Ideas for Using Transitional Words and Phrases

- Collect student writing samples that include transition words. Cover the words with the sticky note strips. Allow students to work with partners to guess what the transition word might be. Ask them to write their guesses above the covered word. Next, they can uncover the words to see if their guesses were correct. As they do this, they may discover that the transition word used may change the meaning of the sentence.

- Make a transparency of an expository paragraph taken from a magazine or newspaper. With highlighting tape, identify the transitional words and phrases used. Instruct students to write a paragraph explaining how to do something that they know a lot about. Challenge them to use transitional words and phrases.

- Identify specific published works where transitional words and phrases are used. Use these as models of how real authors write more effectively by using these words. Here are some examples:

  - *No More Water in the Tub!* by Tedd Arnold (Dial Books for Young Readers, 1995).
    then, so, but, in an instant, then out the door and down the steps (repeated), while, suddenly

  - *Boundless Grace* by Mary Hoffman (Puffin, 2000).
    well, and, then, but, the next day, sometimes, soon, later

  - *The Pig Who Ran a Red Light* by Paul Brett Johnson (Orchard Books, 1999).
    ever since, now, however, when, the following day, after lunch, later that afternoon, suddenly, at last

  - *The Cow Who Wouldn't Come Down* by Paul Brett Johnson (Orchard Books, 1997).
    when, but, finally, sooner or later, then, just as, that evening, next, later

  - *Armadillo Tattletale* by Helen Ketteman (Scholastic, Inc., 2000).
    but, and, one day, when, to this day

  - *The Relatives Came* by Cynthia Rylant (Atheneum, 2001).
    so, then, and finally, but, finally, after a long time, and, while

  - *When I Was Young in the Mountains* by Cynthia Rylant (E.P. Dutton Books, 1982).
    when, later, on our way, afterward

Mini-Lesson Focus: Writing a Paragraph with a Central Idea and Supporting Details

A paragraph includes a group of sentences that are organized around one single main idea. Every detail should support that main idea. Third-grade students often veer off of the topic when writing a paragraph. It is important to teach them to plan before they begin to write.

Tell the students, "As I think about when we had a lesson on writing a complete sentence, I remember that it was so important to answer all the questions to make the sentence complete. Now we are writing paragraphs, and I know that we have to think about how to make the paragraph complete."

Discuss with students the importance of focusing the topic on the main reason they are writing the paragraph. Tell them to be sure to include adequate supporting details to make the paragraph complete.

"Today, I am going to write a paragraph about a visit from my daughter and her friends. I could tell you many things, but I will focus on one of the experiences during the visit. First, I will develop a web that shows some of the experiences we had during the visit."

"Now, I can choose one to write about. I think I will tell you about the sleeping arrangements."

Five Is Enough

Recently my daughter, Susan, and four of her friends came home from college for a weekend visit. My husband and I began to worry about where everyone would sleep. We only have three bedrooms and not enough beds for our guests. All of the extra pillows, blankets, and sleeping bags were rounded up. A pallet on the floor is not hard when these materials are layered. We decided to use my office space as an extra bedroom. This was a good idea. In the end, everyone had a place to sleep. As my daughter and her friends were leaving, we discussed the next visit and we said, "Five is enough!"

Identify the central idea and supporting details in the paragraph. Underline the central idea and number the supporting details. Insert them into a form such as the one below. Explain that each supporting detail must connect back to the central idea.

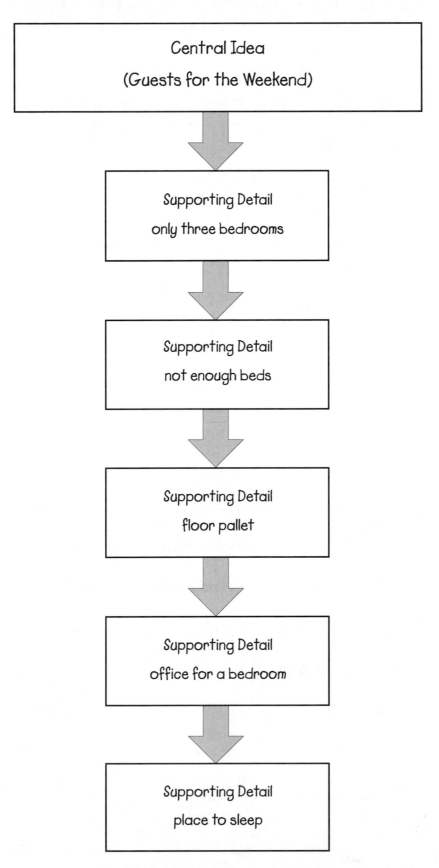

Mini-Lesson Focus: Writing Multiple Paragraphs on the Same Topic

Once students have begun to develop their ideas more fully, they are ready to branch out into multiple paragraph compositions. They'll think it's much harder than it actually is. However, they'll definitely need help from you to keep their paragraphs focused and organized. Let's start with writing informational text that may be easier to organize.

Day One

Tell the students, "We're going to learn to write several good paragraphs on the same topic. We're going to work hard to stay focused and to group our ideas in a way that makes sense."

Determine a topic for your writing, such as the bald eagle. Draw lines on your transparency or paper as in the diagram below. You might start with just a two-paragraph design and add paragraphs later if your students are ready to grow. Write your topic in the top block of the first column.

Topic: Bald Eagles	Notes:
1.	
2.	

Brainstorm with your students a list of questions they would like to know about bald eagles, such as:

- How did they become the national emblem of the United States?

- Where do you find them?

- Why are they endangered?

- How big are they?

- How do they care for their babies?

- How fast do they fly?

Narrow the list to two questions your students are most curious about. Place those questions in the remaining boxes in the first column.

Make notes about what you'll say to answer the questions. For some informational topics, you'll consult a book or reference material. For some topics where you're the "expert," you won't need reference material, but you'll simply make notes.

Topic: Bald Eagles	Notes
1. How did they become the US national emblem?	• 3 men given the task: John Adams, Ben Franklin, Thomas Jefferson, but they were busy (Ben wanted the turkey!) • William Barton drew a design and gave to Congress • Stood for strength and power
2. Why are they endangered?	• DDT sprayed on fields in the 1970s • Went from fields to streams to fish eaten by eagles • Now protected by law; are threatened, not endangered

Day Two

Now model for students how to take the middle row (question 1) and write a paragraph about that question. Then, question 2 becomes the second paragraph. For example, for the first paragraph:

> The bald eagle is the national emblem of the United States. How did the eagle become the national emblem? In 1776, three men were given the task by the new government. Those men were John Adams, Benjamin Franklin, and Thomas Jefferson. Benjamin Franklin wanted to choose a turkey to be the emblem. No one else liked his idea. These men were all busy helping to form the country's new government and never completed the task. A man named William Barton drew a design with a bald eagle and gave it to Congress. They liked his idea! They felt that the eagle stood for strength and power.

As you write the second paragraph, explain to students that paragraphs simply signal that there is a new idea, a new thought, or someone new speaking. The second paragraph might be:

> Bald eagles once were endangered because of an insecticide called DDT that was sprayed on fields in the 1970s. The poison ended up in streams where fish swam. The bald eagles ate these fish and died. Because the government has protected them, the bald eagle is no longer on the endangered list. They are now considered to be threatened and are still protected.

Information on eagles from *The Bald Eagle* by Patricia Ryon Quiri (Children's Press, 1998).

Wow! Organizing for multiple paragraphs is not so difficult after all!

Mini-Lesson Focus: Summarizing and Paraphrasing Information

Writing a summary is much like writing a shortened version of the text. Only the most important information should be included. The summary should be written in the writer's own words that incorporate the main idea and selected details. A summary should be brief. When text is rewritten in different words, it is called paraphrasing the information. Students need to see examples of paraphrasing to understand that this technique is used instead of copying exactly an author's words and using them as their own.

Model a way of taking notes and then writing a paragraph that paraphrases this information. Decide on a topic that is introduced in science or social studies.

Using a journal (notebook or several pages of notebook paper stapled together), write a question about the topic on each page. For example, if the topic is the bald eagle, then the questions might be: **Where do they live? What do they eat? What are their enemies? What do they look like?**

Next, generate resources in which the answers to the questions can be found. Possible resources: trade books, encyclopedia, science book, the Internet, an interview, etc.

When writing the answers, be sure to model taking notes and not copying answers word for word from the text. Write the answers to each question from the different resources. Then, each question with notes becomes the text for each paragraph.

A paragraph is then written, paraphrasing the notes on each page.

Tell the students, "Sometimes I want to write a brief description of an article or book I just read. If I take notes on this information, then I can write a paragraph from my notes and not copy the author's words word for word. I just read about the bald eagle. I read an article and a trade book about this beautiful bird. Some of the factual information can be written in a notebook. I can answer questions such as, "Where do they live?" and "What do they eat?" from each source on different pages. Then, I can use these notes to write."

Notes:

Most eagles live in mountainous areas.

Eagles eat small rodents, insects, etc.

Eagles are large birds and are used as a symbol of freedom in the United States.

Larger, meat-eating animals are the eagle's enemies.

Humans might be considered enemies of eagles, if people hunted eagles.

Show students how, after gathering information into note form, you can create a paragraph that summarizes what you've learned:

Eagles

Eagles are interesting birds. They are very large and often live in mountainous areas. The mountains offer protection for their young, as well as a place from which to swoop down on their prey. They feed on rats and other small animals, and then they give pieces of the meat to their babies. The eagle has to be careful around larger animals because they can be enemies. Some hunters might also be the eagle's enemy. The eagle is a powerful bird and is the United States' symbol of freedom.

Guide the students to note that the paragraph does not consist of what the author said word for word, but instead paraphrases the information from the notes.

Other Suggestions for Summarizing and Paraphrasing Information

• Model how to keep a journal of classroom events. After keeping these notes for a week, write a brief summary of what happened during the week. Assign a class reporter each week to continue the class journal. The students will look forward to their turns!

• Model writing a brief summary at the end of each science or social studies lesson. Discuss the most important facts learned in the lesson. These exit entries make a great source of review for the test. The students can continue this practice by adding summary statements after each lesson to a learning log.

• Model how to use a graphic organizer **after** writing to generate a summary. This example of writing can be a paragraph from the text, a magazine article, or a teacher-generated paragraph. Select an example of writing, then develop a graphic organizer showing the key points. A brief summary of that writing can now be written from the graphic organizer.

References

Professional References

Cunningham, P. M. and Hall, D. P. (1998) *Month-by-Month Phonics for Third Grade.* Greensboro, NC: Carson-Dellosa Publishing Co.

Cunningham, P. M., Hall, D. P., and Cunningham, J. W. (2000) *Guided Reading the Four-Blocks® Way.* Greensboro, NC: Carson-Dellosa Publishing Co.

Cunningham, P. M., Hall, D. P., and Gambrell, L. B. (2002) *Self-Selected Reading the Four-Blocks® Way.* Greensboro, NC: Carson-Dellosa Publishing Co.

Cunningham, P. M., Hall, D. P., and Sigmon, C. M. (1999) *The Teacher's Guide to the Four Blocks®.* Greensboro, NC: Carson-Dellosa Publishing Co.

Children's Works Cited

Agatha's Feather Bed: Not Just Another Wild Goose Story by Carmen Deedy (Peachtree Publishers, 1994).

Amazing Grace by Mary Hoffman (Scott Foresman, 1991).

Amazing Snakes by Alexandra Parsons (Knopf Publishing, 1990).

Animal Defenses: How Animals Protect Themselves by Etta Kaner (Kids Can Press, 1999).

Armadillo Tattletale by Helen Ketteman (Scholastic, Inc., 2000).

The Bald Eagle by Patricia Ryon Quiri (Children's Press, 1998).

Bats by Gail Gibbons (Holiday House, 2000).

Because of Winn-Dixie by Kate DiCamillo (Candlewick Press, 2001).

The Bootmaker and the Elves by Susan Lowell (Orchard Books, 1997).

Boundless Grace by Mary Hoffman (Puffin, 2000).

Bringing the Rain to Kapiti Plain by Verna Aardema (Dial Books for Young Readers, 1990).

Chrysanthemum by Kevin Henkes (Mulberry Books, 1996).

The Cow Who Wouldn't Come Down by Paul Bret Johnson (Orchard Books, 1997).

Harry Potter series by J. K. Rowling (Scholastic, Inc.).

Hunters and Prey by Beatrice McLeod (Blackbirch Press, Inc., 2000).

Jolly Postman series by Janet and Allan Ahlberg (Little, Brown and Co.).

Julius, Baby of the World by Kevin Henkes (Mulberry Books, 1995).

Moonflute by Audrey Wood (Harcourt, 1986).

More Than Anything Else by Marie Bradby (Orchard Books, 1995).

No More Water in the Tub! by Tedd Arnold (Dial Books for Young Readers, 1995).

"The One-Horse Farmer" by Sally Derby (*Spider* magazine, February 1999).

Owen by Kevin Henkes (Greenwillow, 1993).

The Pig Who Ran a Red Light by Paul Brett Johnson (Orchard Books, 1999).

The Relatives Came by Cynthia Rylant (Atheneum, 2001).

Spider the Horrible Cat by Nanette Newman (Harcourt, 1993).

Stellaluna by Janell Cannon (Harcourt, 1993).

The Story of Ruby Bridges by Robert Coles (Scholastic, Inc., 1995).

Stuart Little by E. B. White (HarperCollins Children's Books, 1974).

Superfudge by Judy Blume (Econo-Clad Books, 1999).

Today Was a Terrible Day by Patricia Reilly Giff (Puffin Books, 1980).

Tough Boris by Mem Fox (Voyager Books, 1998).

Tyrannosaurus Rex by Elaine Landau (Children's Press, 1999).

Whales and Dolphins: What They Have in Common by Elizabeth Tayntor Gowell (Franklin Watts, Inc., 2000).

When I Was Young in the Mountains by Cynthia Rylant (E. P. Dutton, 1982).

The White House by Tristan Boyer Binns (Heinemann Library, 2001).

Wilfrid Gordon McDonald Partridge by Mem Fox (Kane/Miller Book Publishers, 1995).

Yours Truly, Goldilocks by Alma Flor Ada (Atheneum, 1998).

Notes

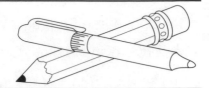

Writing Mini-Lessons for Third Grade: The Four-Blocks® Model